# FORT HENRY

## AN ILLUSTRATED HISTORY

Stephen D. Mecredy

Photography by Jeffrey Chiang and Jack Chiang

Foreword by Peter Trueman

JAMES LORIMER & COMPANY LTD., PUBLISHERS

TORONTO

James Lorimer & Company Ltd. acknowledges the support of the Ontario Arts Council. We acknowledge the financial support of the Government of Canada through the Book Publishing Industry Development Program (BPIDP) for our publishing activities. We acknowledge the support of the Canada Council for the Arts for our publishing program.

Canadian Cataloguing in Publication Data

Mecredy, Stephen D. (Stephen David), 1955–
          Fort Henry: an illustrated history

Includes index.
ISBN 1-55028-631-5

1. Fort Henry (Ont.) – History. I. Title.

FC3099.K5Z57 2000          971.3'72          C99-932848-4
F1059.5K5M42 2000

James Lorimer & Company Ltd., Publishers
35 Britain St.
Toronto, Ontario
M5A 1R7

Printed and bound in Canada.

# PHOTO CREDITS

Except for the following images, all photographs in this book were taken either by Jeffrey Chiang or Jack Chiang.

Anne S. K. Brown Military Collection: 41, 47; Baldwin Room, Toronto Reference Library: 45; Fort Henry National Historic Site: 35, 43, 44 (left & right), 46, 48, 49, 51 (top & bottom), 52, 53, 55, 56, 57 (bottom), 59, 60, 61, 63; Marine Museum of the Great Lakes at Kingston: 40 (bottom) Stephen Mecredy: 13; National Archives of Canada: 9, 38 (top), 42 (top & bottom); Parks Canada: 39 (bottom), 40 (top); Royal Military College, Kingston: 38 Ernie Sparks: 6

The editors wish to thank Ron Dale at Niagara National Historic Sites for drawing our attention to the Anne S. K. Brown Military Collection; Ron Ridley, Curator of Fort Henry, for his tireless work in assembling historical images from the fort, and also Preston Schiedel, who carefully reshot many of these images.

Every effort has been made to trace the ownership of all copyrighted material reproduced in this book. We regret any errors and will be pleased to make any necessary corrections in future editions.

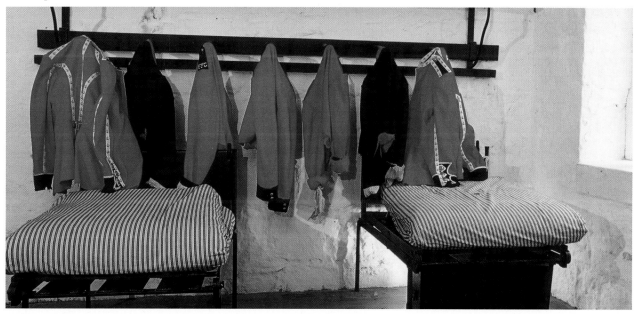

# CONTENTS

# FOREWORD

Kingston is an institutional town, given a distinctive flavour by its penitentiaries, Queen's University, government agencies, the town's churches, hospitals, the Royal Military College, and a sprawling Canadian forces base adjacent to Fort Henry. The town has had a pervasive military presence from the time the French put troops here and set up a trading post in 1673.

That first fort, Cataraqui, was replaced by Fort Frontenac, which the British captured in 1758. Fortifications were raised on Point Henry during the War of 1812, but Fort Henry in its present form wasn't completed until 1837. Before highways and railroads, the Great Lakes and the St. Lawrence River were the only transportation corridors through the wilderness, and it was at Kingston that these two corridors met.

Later, the completion of the Rideau Canal made Kingston an even more important commercial junction. When Britain built up her military and naval strength here in the nineteenth century, it was to defend against any interruption of these vital supply routes by the forces of the new American republic.

Those critical of the money spent to build Fort Henry — 88,000 pounds sterling, or about $50,000,000 in current dollars — were quick to point out that its garrison never had to fire a shot in anger. Its defenders, then and now, say this only proved the fort's effectiveness as a deterrent, which is what it was supposed to be. We could hardly have a better person to recount the fort's history than Stephen Mecredy, who has worked inside its walls for more than two decades.

After the American Civil War, the introduction of rifled, breech-loading guns made the fort obsolete, and it was used only as a storage depot. By the 1930s, when the fort's tourist potential was finally recognized, it was falling to pieces. Its restoration, as a depression works project, cost $827,692.

Today, the fort remains a tourist attraction, and although Kingston is no longer of strategic

*Officers and NCOs of the Fort Henry Guard*

significance, the military is still an important component of everyday life here. Fort Henry, brooding on its hilltop across Kingston harbour, is the dominant symbol of an ancient, ongoing relationship.

Kingston has long had reason to be happy with its military establishment. During the war of 1812, American forces attacked and occupied the town of York, now Toronto. The British believed Kingston would be next, and strengthened the modest emplacements on Point Henry, the site of the present fort. American troops, poised to strike from Sacketts Harbour across the lake, concluded Kingston was too well defended and turned to easier targets down the St. Lawrence.

Again during the Rebellions of 1837, Kingstonians found they owed a debt of gratitude to their military protectors. When the first uprising took place in Lower Canada, now Quebec, the British administration in Toronto, believing there would be no trouble there, stripped Upper Canada of her regular forces to support those stationed in French Canada. As a result, when another rebellion broke out north of Toronto, the new Fort Henry, then nearing completion, was manned only by ordnance personnel and a few seamen.

Luckily for Kingston, Major Richard Bonnycastle of the Royal Engineers was the senior British officer present. Like other engineer officers, he had earned his commission, not

*Royal Sappers and Miners, 1832*

purchased it. Much was expected of such men. Their jobs were complex, their responsibilities were enormous, and Bonnycastle, at 46, was a seasoned veteran. He responded swiftly and effectively to orders from Sir Francis Bond Head, Lieutenant-Governor of Upper Canada, to hold Fort Henry against the rebels.

With enthusiasm and tact, he set about building a garrison from the little he had available. By the beginning of 1838, he had armed the artisans and labourers used to build the fort, recruited nearby Mohawks, brought in militia from the area around Kingston, and encouraged townspeople to join the Frontenac Light Dragoons. In addition, he'd secured the services of a detachment of the Perth Artillery, and set up a unit of naval gunners as the Queen's Marine Artillery.

Meanwhile, a couple of thousand Upper Canadian rebels and American sympathizers had gathered at Clayton, New York, across the frozen St. Lawrence, with the idea of attacking and taking Fort Henry. They made a preliminary foray towards Gananoque, and seized Hickory Island. But when their scouts reconnoitered the fort's now formidable defences, the rebels wisely withdrew.

Overjoyed, the citizens of Kingston credited Major Bonnycastle with staving off the attack. London was in agreement, apparently, and he was knighted in 1840. Sir Richard, who came to regard the place

*Ballroom dancing in the parade ground*

as home, died in Kingston as a lieutenant-colonel in 1847.

Bonnycastle was by no means the last military man to put down roots here. Many officers and enlisted men who have served at C.F.B. Kingston, Royal Military College or the Staff College, return when they retire from the armed forces. With many other Kingstonians, they make an appreciative audience for the sunset ceremonies and military tattoos held on the parade square of the old fort.

But Fort Henry is not just a monument to the town's military traditions. It is often used for civic celebrations and other worthy causes. My first experience with the fort was when Kingston's own Tragically Hip staged a fund-raising concert there in support of Almost Home, a charitable project with which I was associated.

At one point in the evening, I stood up to stretch my legs and found myself leaning against the solid stone wall of the fort. To my astonishment, the wall of sound being generated by the Tragically Hip and their amplifiers had the apparently immovable stone rocking and vibrating between my shoulder blades, as if the fort's guns were bombarding an advancing enemy.

The decibel levels of 1990s music would never have been dreamed of in 1938, when the man in charge of Fort Henry's restoration, and its director until 1965, Ronald Way, instituted the Fort Henry Guard. The Guard, which

*Children on parade*

is still impressing visitors today, demonstrates the British army's drill and fighting formations during the old fort's heyday, about 1860. Way's idea was that the Guard would breathe life into the "Old Stones." They do. But so did the Tragically Hip, believe me!

The fort is a multifaceted asset. In addition to everything else, for example, it provides a window on the lives of ordinary people in the 1860s, recalling the social gap that existed between the officer-class and common soldiers. The size of the wine cellar for the officers' mess (about 10 feet by 20 feet) and the size of a cell for privates under punishment (8 feet by 3 feet) tell us as much about British and colonial society in general as it does about life in the army.

Until early 1999, Fort Henry was administered by the Department of National Defence. Now, fittingly perhaps for an establishment more than a century beyond any danger of active military service, it is under the protective wing of Parks Canada.

"Drum-and-trumpet history" is a phrase sometimes used by commentators to denigrate any account of past events deemed to have given undue prominence to battles and wars. But Old Fort Henry could never be dismissed as a "drum-and-trumpet fort." As Mr. Mecredy's fascinating history makes clear, Fort Henry's legacy is essentially one of peace.

Peter Trueman

# INTRODUCTION

Fort Henry National Historic Site is one of Canada's premier historic attractions. Restored to the 1860s, the fort welcomes friends and former foes alike to take part in and enjoy part of Canada's illustrious past. The Fort Henry Guard brings the fort to life each summer and offers visitors an opportunity to travel back in time to 1867.

The fort was first built during the War of 1812, then redesigned and rebuilt in the 1830s and, finally, restored in the 1930s. Over the years, its only successful enemies have been indifference and neglect. Throughout much of the nineteenth century, Fort Henry was indeed the "Citadel of Upper Canada" as it stood on the promontory overlooking Kingston's commercial and naval harbour and the entrance to the Rideau Canal.

Advances in weapons technology in the 1860s, specifically the advent of rifled breech-loading guns, made the fort obsolete. Luckily for future generations, the 65 acres (26.3 hectares) of land on which Fort Henry sits has always

View North-east from Kingston Harbour to Points Frederick and Henry, c. 1838, *by W.H. Bartlett*

been under the jurisdiction of either Great Britain or the Government of Canada; consequently, this prime piece of real estate was never commercially developed.

The history of Fort Henry marched in step with the history of Canada in its early years. From the War of 1812 up to and including Confederation in 1867, the fort was part of national events. The existing fort was built in response to the cold war of distrust between Great Britain and the United States in the 1820s and 1830s. During the 1846–47 Oregon Boundary Crisis and the 1860–65 American Civil War, British troop levels were increased and significant military building took place to strengthen the defences in Kingston.

Following the Civil War, the fort's importance waned significantly as relations between the new Dominion of Canada and the United States improved. At first, the fort became a school of gunnery. When the North-West Rebellion broke out in 1885, the local Princess of Wales Own Rifles garrisoned the fort as well. During both World Wars Fort Henry was an

*The east ditch tower, with the Martello tower on Cedar Island in the distance*

internment camp, initially for so-called "enemy aliens" and later for Enemy Merchant Seamen and Prisoners of War.

Interestingly, Fort Henry's insignificance in the grand scheme of Canada's defence in the late nineteenth and early twentieth centuries proved to be its salvation in the long run. Had Kingston and the fort been of ongoing defensive importance, the fort probably would have been replaced or significantly upgraded. As it was, after the 1860s, the fort was left to the devices of time and the weather. The restoration that began in the 1930s is one of the most remarkable aspects of the fort's history. It was the first time the Government of Canada agreed to work with the Government of Ontario in the field of historic restoration. In 1936–1938 this was a new and innovative concept. The Canadian government would not undertake another restoration of this magnitude for another twenty-five years.

The history of Fort Henry is also about people — some famous, but most unnamed. Canada's first prime minister, Sir John A. Macdonald, was involved in two important trials in the late 1830s that concerned people and events in the fort. Major Richard Bonnycastle "saved" the town during the Rebellions and later returned to build the distinctive Martello towers for which Kingston is so famous. He was also a noted writer in his time. Fort Henry Bates was the first child born at the current fort and his descendants carried the Henry name for several

generations. We know that Major Burt was the fort's commanding officer during much of the American Civil War, but thousands of unnamed soldiers garrisoned the fort and carried out the monotonous daily routine throughout the 1800s. Nick Sakaliuk was imprisoned as an "enemy alien" in the First World War, as were thousands of others; Henry Strehl was one of many prisoners of war housed in Camp 31, Fort Henry POW camp in the Second World War. Ronald Way's name must also be noted as the man behind the restoration of Fort Henry and the father of historic restoration in Canada.

In the end it is people that bring structures to life. The legacy of Way and others is the Fort Henry Guard, the group of men and women who breathe life into Fort Henry today in remembrance of those who garrisoned this important outpost of the British Empire in the nineteenth century.

*File firing in the parade square*

# MAP

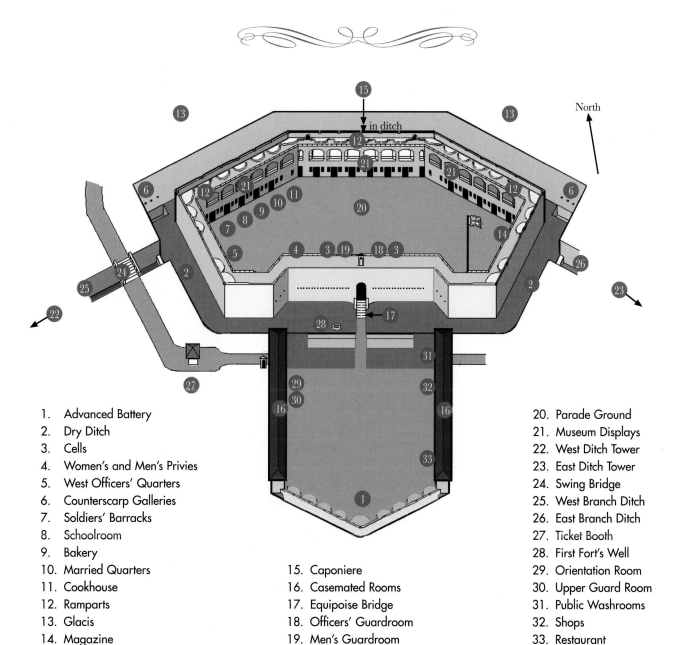

1. Advanced Battery
2. Dry Ditch
3. Cells
4. Women's and Men's Privies
5. West Officers' Quarters
6. Counterscarp Galleries
7. Soldiers' Barracks
8. Schoolroom
9. Bakery
10. Married Quarters
11. Cookhouse
12. Ramparts
13. Glacis
14. Magazine

15. Caponiere
16. Casemated Rooms
17. Equipoise Bridge
18. Officers' Guardroom
19. Men's Guardroom

20. Parade Ground
21. Museum Displays
22. West Ditch Tower
23. East Ditch Tower
24. Swing Bridge
25. West Branch Ditch
26. East Branch Ditch
27. Ticket Booth
28. First Fort's Well
29. Orientation Room
30. Upper Guard Room
31. Public Washrooms
32. Shops
33. Restaurant

# 1

# A TOUR OF FORT HENRY

Kingston was established at the confluence of three waterways, Lake Ontario, the Rideau Canal to Ottawa, and the St. Lawrence River, which flows to Montreal and eventually the Atlantic Ocean. Military arms and equipment, civilian goods, and people all moved along these nineteenth century highways and regularly had to stop in Kingston. Smaller craft were used along the St.

Lawrence and the Rideau while large sailing ships and steamers plied the waters of Lake Ontario. Consequently, Kingston became a convenient transshipment point for everything moving up or down these waters.

Fort Henry is strategically situated atop Point Henry, the highest ground in Kingston. The fort was built to defend the "Dock Yard and Naval and Commercial

*Fort Henry as it appears today*

*The advanced battery*

Harbour of Kingston" according to the language of the day. The dockyard was located on Point Frederick, which is currently the location of the Royal Military College of Canada, while the naval and commercial harbour lined the shores of Kingston.

Technically speaking, Fort Henry is a five-sided casemated redoubt. A redoubt is a self-contained fortification that cannot cover its flanks, or walls, from its own parapets. The parapets are the tops of the walls, built over the rooms or casemates. Casemates are individual, bombproof rooms with vaulted ceilings constructed of many layers of brick. Since the defenders on the parapets could not see the ditch directly in front of them, a system of counterscarp galleries and caponieres was built so that they could shoot at the enemy if they got into the ditch.

The tour below follows the one offered by Fort Henry's interpreters and discusses all major points of interest.

## Advanced Battery

A group of guns placed together for a particular purpose is called a battery and the fort's advanced battery takes its name from the guns which sit in front of, or in advance of, the main redoubt. The battery was completed by 1837, at the same time as the redoubt. Without it, the fort would have been defenceless from an attack by water since none of the fort's other guns faced south towards Lake Ontario. The battery comprised nine 32-pounder smoothbore muzzle loading guns, each capable of firing a 32-pound (16 kilogram) shot accurately about 800 yards (730 metres) into Kingston harbour.

In 1843 a series of twenty-two casemated rooms, each measuring 18 feet by 30 feet (5.5 by 9.1 metres) in the form of two long, narrow, eleven-room buildings, were completed. They connect the battery of guns with the redoubt,

*The bombproof casemates of the advanced battery*

getting close to the walls of the redoubt. The depth of the ditch made it very difficult for anyone to simply jump in — ladders would have had to be lowered into the ditch for the men to climb down. While men were climbing into the ditch, or standing in it, they would be subject to a murderous hail of bullets from soldiers inside the fort firing through the 302 loopholes which look out into the ditch.

One of the more interesting features of the ditch is the first fort's well. The well is on the west side as you enter the ditch from the advanced battery. It is the only structure that still remains from the initial fort. The southeast and southwest corners of the ditch are rounded in order to deflect shot from the counterscarp galleries in its northern corners. In the middle of the northern section of the ditch, a small building known as a caponiere was built. It eliminated an area of dead ground where the enemy could not be seen, and created a deadly crossfire with the galleries in the northeast and northwest corners of the counterscarp.

completely walling off the fort from outside. These bombproof casemates were constructed in a similar style to all the rooms in the fort, with a vaulted ceiling made of eight to ten layers of brick. These ceilings were relatively bombproof against the existing smoothbore artillery fire of the day and provided the fort's storage and inhabitants a safe and secure haven in the event of attack. The buildings were topped with a distinctive tin roof, painted red, and readily seen from outside the fort.

## The Dry Ditch

Fort Henry was well defended from long range attack from both land and water. However, if these defences failed, the fort was protected from close attack as well. The main redoubt is completely surrounded by a dry ditch approximately 40 feet wide and 30 feet deep (12 by 9 metres). The ditch exists between the wall of the redoubt (the escarp) and another wall 40 feet (12 metres) away (the counterscarp). The purpose of the ditch was to prevent the enemy from

*The dry ditch and main gate*

## Cells and Privies

Obedience was a very important part of the British army. For soldiers who were disobedient, there was always some form of punishment. Confinement was the most common form of punishment and for this, Fort Henry was fitted with ten 8 by 3 foot (9 by 2.4 metre) cells. The most frequent crime a soldier committed was to be drunk and disorderly. Alcoholism was a serious problem in the army and soldiers often spent time in the fort's cells drying out.

Regulations stated that a soldier could not be kept in the fort's cells for longer than forty-two days. If his crime merited further punishment, he was sent to the Kingston Penitentiary, which was opened in 1838. There were no military prisons in Canada at the time. By the 1860s flogging was rarely if ever used.

If a soldier deserted he would be branded or tattooed with the letter D under his upper arm. If the man was an habitual offender he might be drummed out of the regiment, but before that he would be tattooed with the letters BC for bad character, again under the upper arm. This branding was very painful.

The fort's privies were divided into men's, women's, and officers'. The men's and women's privies were next to each other in divided rooms and separated outside by a wooden screen which provided a bit of privacy. The officers' privies were located under the stairs in the southeast and southwest corners of the fort in the demi-bastions.

Interestingly, the women's privy, which was used by the garrison children, had seats while the men's did not. All the privies were scrubbed daily by soldiers' wives who took turns cleaning and were paid a bit of money for their trouble. The boys used the men's when they were old enough to hold on to the railings to prevent themselves from falling in. Whenever it rained, water was collected in drains located around the fort's large parade square and flushed through the privies. The effluent flowed through a two-foot square brick and stone "pipe" down into Navy Bay, just beside the fort. In the 1860s the privies were flushed occasionally by a fire engine.

*An 8 by 3 foot cell*

*The men's privies*

## West Officers' Quarters

Accommodation for officers at Fort Henry was located in the east and west walls of the fort and was luxurious compared to a private soldier's. There were six casemates in the east wall for officers, while the west wall had four additional officers' quarters, as well as an anteroom,

*Officer's quarters, interior*

officers' mess, messman's room and that most important of rooms, the wine cellar. All the casemates measured about 18 by 30 feet (5.5 by 9.1 meters). Today, the west officers' quarters is open to the public and furnished as it might have looked in 1867.

Of the officers in the British army in 1867, approximately 15 per cent came from the aristocracy, 15 per cent had fathers who had been officers in the military, and 65 per cent came from families of the minor nobility, the clergy, and the relatively well-off middle class. In wartime, promotions could be rapid, as there was a high mortality rate among officers. In

peacetime, promotion was by seniority in the artillery and engineers and by purchase (for those who could afford it) in the cavalry and the infantry.

To be promoted in the cavalry or infantry, an officer usually had to have served a certain number of years in each particular rank and then be in a position to purchase the higher rank when it became available. Prices for ranks, in what was known as the "Purchase System," varied based on supply and demand and the popularity of a particular regiment. Officers in the artillery and engineers, however, went to the Royal Military Academy at Woolwich, England. Upon graduation they were commissioned. The Royal Military College at Sandhurst opened in 1812 and by the 1860s many infantry and cavalry officers had also attended the college prior to purchasing their first commission.

*Officer's quarters, showing bath*

*Officers' anteroom*

Officers often rented lodgings in the town of Kingston, particularly if they were married. They kept their room at the fort for an office and as a place to stay in the event of war. Officers were responsible for furnishing their lodgings at the fort at their own expense.

The officers' anteroom served as a library, a gamesroom, and an area for entertaining guests before and after dinner in the mess. The anteroom and the mess were furnished by the officers and were often quite lavish. The piano in the fort's anteroom was built at the Fox Piano Factory in Kingston in the 1860s and is

*Fox piano in the Officers' anteroom*

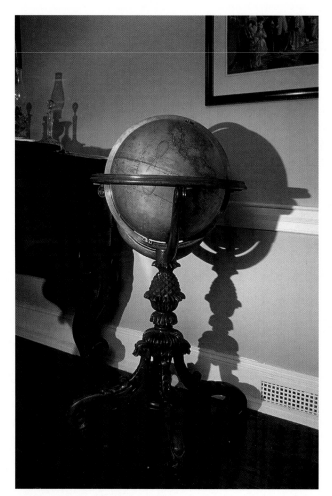

*Original globe in the Officers' anteroom*

but forbidden in the mess. Unless they had specific duties requiring their attention, all officers were expected to attend the evening meal. Sometimes married officers were given permission to miss a few meals a week so that they could dine with their wives at homes in Kingston.

The Messman was hired by the officers to prepare their meals and supervise each officer's soldier servant. He could be a former senior non-commissioned officer from the army, but was often a civilian trained in the cooking and serving arts. The Messman lived and worked in the messman's room in the west officers' quarters, right next to the wine cellar. The officers ate very well. The Messman and a servant or two travelled into Kingston nearly every day to purchase the food required. In addition, sometimes small vegetable gardens were kept in the fort's ditch to augment both the officers' and the men's daily cuisine.

Officers were gentlemen, and as such, it was assumed that they could be trusted to drink responsibly. They were permitted to purchase alcohol and keep it in their quarters, a luxury the private soldier was not afforded. The officers also paid a certain amount each month into the mess fund to pay for the Messman, the food, and the alcohol consumed in the mess.

Officers entertained at the fort and were entertained in town by the upper classes of Kingston society. The newspapers of the day are full of detailed descriptions of the social events in which officers took part, including formal balls, theatrical presentations, skating parties, and tobogganing on Fort Henry hill. Many of Kingston's finest young

*Original Officer's coatee, c. 1828–55*

typical of the kinds of furnishings that were in the room at the time. The room also features a large composite photograph of the officers of the Royal Canadian Rifle Regiment (RCRR), the unit that garrisoned Fort Henry the longest.

The tradition of the mess in the British army was a strong one. The officers' mess was well furnished so the officers could eat in style for their primary meal of the day, supper. They sat down to eat, almost anywhere in the world, on fine bone china, spotless crystal, and sterling silver trays. Their conversation was often limited to such topics as hunting, sport, horses, and trivia. Topics such as sex, women, politics, religion and what we would call shop talk were all ladies lost their hearts to one of Her Majesty's officers. The upper class social life of Kingston was greatly improved by the presence of the British army.

## Counterscarp Galleries (The Reverse Fire Chambers)

For any fort to be successful it had to be able to defend its own walls or flanks. Fort Henry was no exception to this rule and in addition to the loopholes that look into the ditch from nearly every casemate in the fort, there were six small casemates built into the northeast and northwest walls, or counterscarps, of the ditch. These counterscarp galleries were quite innovative when the fort was built. They were 15 to 20 feet (or about 5 metres) underground, could not be shot at by an attacker, and enabled those inside them to shoot at anyone in the ditch, by setting up a murderous crossfire in conjunction with the men firing from the loopholes.

In the first three galleries, soldiers alone were expected to maintain a continuous fire out through the four loopholes. An 18-pounder carronade was intended to be set up in each of the next three rooms. For some reason, only two carronades were ever placed here. The carronades were built to fire a shot that weighed 18 pounds (8 kilograms), but in the confined space of the ditch, they would have fired canister. Canister shot looked like a large can filled with small round balls or shot, each one about the size of a golf ball. When the carronade fired, the canister holding the shot disintegrated

and the balls spread out and filled the width of the ditch, mowing down anyone in their path. The carronades in the galleries are original, as are their wooden carriages.

*Inside the counterscarp galleries*

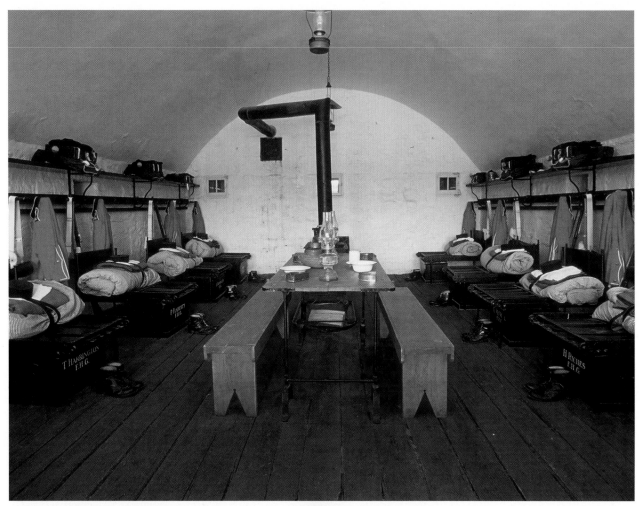

*Soldiers' barrack room in one of the fort's casemates*

## Soldiers' Barracks

The lifestyle of the regular soldiers or "other ranks" as they were known was quite different from that of the officers. Officers had their own quarters whereas eleven soldiers shared a casemate slightly bigger than one officer's quarter. Officers had soldier servants; the other ranks did not. Officers could keep and consume alcohol in their quarters; the other ranks could not. Officers paid for their own food and their cook to prepare it; the other ranks did not.

*Badges of rank*

These rooms measure 18 by 36 feet (5.5 by 11 metres) and today contain reproduction furniture and accoutrements like those used by the rank and file of the British Army in 1867. The soldiers slept, ate, and spent most of their off-duty time in their barrack room. The room became their home and their barrack mates their family. Each man was issued a bed, a straw-filled mattress, sheets, a blanket, and one barrack box in which he could keep his few personal belongings. His uniform and accoutrements were placed on hooks behind the bed in a specific place and order. Barrack rooms were inspected once a day to insure they were clean and orderly. The importance of cleanliness was probably lost on the soldiers, but the military knew that a barrack room cleaned and scrubbed almost 365 days a year prevented illness and disease. With eleven men to a room, illness and disease could spread like wildfire. During the 1847 typhoid fever epidemic in Kingston, the army "retreated" to their clean barracks at Tête du Pont and Fort Henry and kept to themselves. Not one soldier's life was lost as a result while nearly 2,000 civilians died.

Generally, barracks were poorly lit, heated, and ventilated. The oppressive smell of eleven men sharing one room need only be imagined. In addition, a urine tub was placed in the room for the men's convenience during the night. There are many accounts of non-commissioned officers opening a barracks to wake the soldiers in the morning and being repulsed by the smell emanating from the room.

Sickness was a problem for the army, in spite of the preventative steps taken. Sicknesses related to the soldiers' living conditions, such as tuberculosis, respiratory ailments, and fevers, were responsible for the hospitalization of 37 per cent of the ranks in 1860. In Canada conditions were better and there were 50 per cent fewer hospitalizations than in Britain.

Unlike the officers, soldiers did not purchase their rank. The enlisted soldier usually came from the lower classes of British society, the "scum of the earth" as the Duke of Wellington named them.

A soldier's lot was a harsh one, but when compared with what he might have endured in civilian life, the army was often a better place to be. With the exception of having to go to war occasionally, a soldier could be assured of having a roof over his head, regular food to eat, and a bed with sheets and a blanket. In addition, his clothing and necessaries were provided at very little cost. Granted, a soldier was not going to get rich on his pay of a shilling a day less stoppages (the money the army deducted from a soldier's wages to pay for his food and some of his clothing). However, the army provided regular work and if a soldier worked hard and stayed out of trouble he could eventually get promoted and do well for himself.

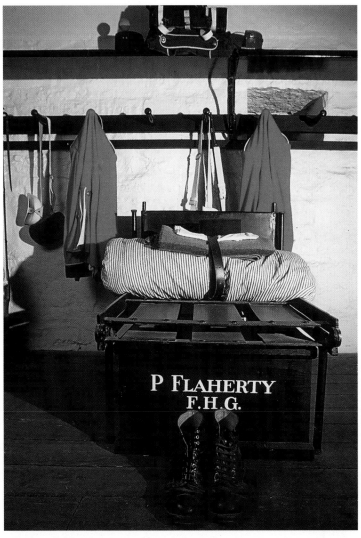

*A soldier's bed, barrack box, uniform, and accoutrements*

*Soldier's shako*

# Schoolroom

The British army cared a great deal about the education of its soldiers and their children. It was believed that educated soldiers would be more effective. In many ways the army was well ahead of British and Canadian civil authorities in its attitudes towards public education, particularly for the lower classes. In 1867 every soldier in the army married "on the strength," which meant with his Commanding Officer's

*The schoolroom*

permission, had to send his children to military school in the barracks until the child was fourteen. This was true for boys and girls alike. In addition, soldiers, especially younger ones, had to attend school in order to learn to read and write. By the 1860s a soldier had to be competent in reading and writing before he could be promoted from Private to

*Children in uniform*

Corporal. Schoolmasters and schoolmistresses in these schools were usually trained at the army school in Chelsea, England.

At Fort Henry the school was divided into "infants" and "grown children." In the morning the infants, nine and under, were under the care and instruction of the school-mistress while the older children, ten to fourteen, worked with the schoolmaster. In the afternoon the older girls went with the schoolmistress and learned valuable domestic skills such as knitting, tatting, and sewing. Both the older boys and girls underwent a strict course of instruction that included reading, writing, dictation, singing, grammar, English history, geography, arithmetic, and algebra.

Once children reached the age of fourteen, they were no longer kept "on the strength" and had to fend for themselves. Boys had the option of joining the army as drummer boys, leaving their families and being apprenticed to a tradesman in Kingston or perhaps becoming child labourers. Girls could usually find work in Kingston as servants.

## Bakery

Bread is the staff of life in any army. For the soldiers at Fort Henry, the daily ration consisted of 1 1/2 pounds (680 grams) of bread per day, along with 3/4 pound (340 grams) of meat, and 1 pound (450 grams) of potatoes; 1/3 ounce (9 grams) of coffee, 1/6 ounce (4.7 grams) of tea, 2 ounces (5.6 grams) of sugar, 1/2 ounce (1.4 grams) of salt, and 1/36 ounce of pepper. Bread was baked in the fort's ovens every day. The baker, usually a soldier, would rise early in the morning and build a fire inside the brick lined ovens. When the bricks were hot enough, the soot would flake off and the baker would slide the loaves into the oven with a long-handled wooden peel. The radiant heat from the bricks cooked the bread, with the first batch taking about 45 minutes. If the baker worked quickly, a second batch could be cooked without lighting another fire in the oven.

Sometimes the soldiers received permission to plant vegetable gardens in the fort's ditch. Detachments of the Royal Canadian Rifle Regiment garrisoned at the fort in the 1850s and 1860s planted gardens with seeds sent from England. After 1857, an extra 3 1/2 pence per soldier was allotted from the regimental funds to augment their daily food. Soldiers usually pooled these meagre funds to buy extra rations and shared the food amongst themselves in the form of stews and soups.

*The bakery*

*Married quarters with blankets for privacy*

## Married Quarters

Very few soldiers were married. The British army was of the opinion that marriage was bad for soldiers and regulations stated that only 6 per cent of the regiment was permitted to be married "on the strength." This rule did not apply to officers. The 6 per cent were usually soldiers with seniority. According to the regulations, soldiers' wives had to be of "good character" and often had to get a letter from their local clergyman saying just that. At foreign stations like Fort Henry, commanding officers often

increased the number of men married on the strength to 12 percent. If a man married "off the strength," his wife had to live out of the barracks and away from her husband who would have to sneak out to see her. The soldier was in serious trouble if his superiors ever found out about his illicit marriage.

Marrying on the strength had significant advantages. A soldier's wife and family were housed in barracks and fed for free. The soldier's wife received half as much food as her husband and any children received one quarter of their father's ration up to the age of fourteen, when they were cut off the strength.

*A costumed interpreter*

Up until the 1850s married couples slept in a corner of the men's barrack room. After the Crimean War (1854–56) separate married quarters began to appear throughout the British Empire. By 1867 the married quarters at Fort Henry consisted of a regular soldiers' barracks sectioned off into three or four separate areas — one for each of the families living there. Bedposts with blankets strung between them provided some privacy in the evening. During the daytime, these blankets had to be tied back for inspection. No single soldiers shared this room. In addition, the fort's ditch towers were used as married quarters for trustworthy soldiers, with one family per each of the three floors in the tower.

Married women on the strength worked hard at Fort Henry. They were responsible for keeping their barracks clean and having them ready for inspection every morning, scrubbing the men's and women's privies (for which they were paid), and doing their wash every Monday. Women were often paid extra for doing an unmarried soldier's wash, sewing, and mending.

Women whose husbands died often remarried within the regiment rather quickly. If they chose not to remarry, they were put on the Widows and Orphans List for three months and then the army made arrangements to transport them back to their home parish in Britain at public expense. If a woman decided she wanted to remain in Canada, she and any of her children were struck off strength and left to find their own way. Finding a husband within the regiment was never difficult, however, and most women remarried as a means of survival for themselves and their children.

## The Cookhouse

Number 1 Cookhouse is one of two rooms in the fort that were used to cook food for the other ranks and their families. Number 2 Cookhouse is located just east of Number 2 Passageway. Officers' food was prepared for them in the officers' kitchen located at the entrance to the counterscarp galleries. The regulations stated that a soldier was entitled

*Number 1 Cookhouse*

*A 24-pounder gun on the east battery ramparts*

was served around noon. The beef and potatoes for each mess or barracks room was put in a mesh bag and labelled so that every mess would get its proper allotment. The bags would all be put in the cauldron and boiled along with any other seasonal vegetables the men had procured. One man per mess was designated as the barrack orderly for the day. It was his job to prepare a table for each meal, go down to the cookhouse, get the food (bread, stew, coffee, etc.) for each meal, bring it back to the barrack room, serve it, and clean up and return the pots and serving items to the cookhouse.

The job of company cook and assistant company cook rotated among the unmarried soldiers of the garrison and was under the supervision of a trained Serjeant cook. The duties began after the evening meal on Saturday, lasted for one week, and included cooking all meals and having them ready on time, cleaning the cookhouse and all its contents, and accompanying the Mess Corporal on his daily trip into Kingston to purchase groceries for the day. The quality of food in the army was rather poor. However it was slightly better in Canada, and it was at least as good, if not better than what lower class British civilians were eating. By 1867 soldiers' wives worked together and prepared meals for their families in Number 2 Cookhouse.

to a daily ration of 3/4 pound (340 grams) of beef. This weight was measured out in bulk and included bone and gristle. In the cookhouse, iron cauldrons were used to cook primarily beef stews and soups. The main meal of the day prepared meals for their families in Number 2 Cookhouse.

If soldiers were hungry in the evenings or just looking to socialize in a non-alcoholic environment, they could go to the dry canteen located in a casemate in the fort's north wall.

## The Ramparts

Fort Henry was built facing north. If the Americans attacked, they would probably have crossed the St. Lawrence somewhere downriver east of Kingston where the water narrowed. Once the crossing was made, troops would have marched on the town and laid siege to the fortress on Point Henry. The nineteen 24-pounder guns firing from the north wall would have made it very difficult for the enemy to keep up an artillery bombardment from afar. 24-pounders fired a cast iron ball weighing 24 pounds (11 kilograms) at a maximum range of 2,230 yards (2,000

*The west ditch tower*

*Firing from the ramparts at night*

men could step up, see over the wall, fire out at the enemy, and then step back down to load under cover.

The northeast corner was the most exposed section of the fort because of the topography of that part of the hill. Consequently, authorities decided to increase the firepower in that corner in 1863 when the 24-pounder was replaced by a larger, more powerful 8-inch shell gun. The shell gun was in turn replaced by an even larger gun in 1875 when a 7-inch breech-loading rifled Armstrong gun was mounted in the corner. The Armstrong gun could fire a projectile weighing 110 pounds (50 kilograms).

When looking out over the east and west ramparts, the fort's branch ditch towers are quite noticeable. These towers were built in 1846–48 and closed off the branch ditches to the water. In each tower a 24-pounder gun sat on the top floor and with the removal of the roof, the guns could swivel in a 360 degree radius to sweep the water and the glacis running up to the fort. The walls of the towers were constructed somewhat elliptically, with the side nearest the fort being quite thin while the side facing the water is quite thick. The reason for this was that if the towers were captured, the fort's guns could easily destroy them, so that their rooftop guns could not be trained on the fort proper.

The fort's south wall did not support any guns. The guns of the advanced battery were deemed sufficient to protect the fort from any attack from the water.

metres) and an effective range of about 1,200 yards (1,100 metres). Common military tactics of the day prescribed digging parallel trenches and tunnels to bring the attackers closer to the fort. However, the lack of topsoil over the limestone and granite bedrock so prevalent in the area would have made digging almost impossible. If the enemy could not be kept at a distance with the 24 pound solid shot, the gunners would switch ammunition to canister shot which was very effective against masses of advancing troops at distances of 200 to 500 yards (or 183 to 460 metres). In addition, the ramparts were constructed with a firing step between the gun emplacements so the infantry-

* * *

To walk through Fort Henry is to take a step back in time to 1867. You are witness to the lives and activities of the British Army in Canada protecting Britain's empire. Daily life in the British garrisons was very similar throughout Canada.

# 2
# FORT HENRY TODAY

*The Corps of Drums*

Fort Henry has been opened every summer since 1948 as a living history museum and historic site. What set the fort apart initially, and what continues to impress visitors today, is the Fort Henry Guard. The Guard was the brainchild of Ronald Way, the fort's Director from 1936 to 1965, and it was a truly revolution-

ary concept when first introduced in 1938. Putting costumed interpreters on the site to inform and entertain visitors was very new at that time. Today interpreters are essential at virtually every major historic site.

The Guard represents the British army in Canada in 1867. The year 1867 was chosen as the date to interpret for two reasons. First, Way felt that the year in which Canada became a nation should be commemorated. Second, the British army converted from the 150-year-old "Brown Bess" musket to the Snider-Enfield breech-loading rifle in 1867 and Way thought it would be a good weapon to interpret. It didn't hurt that the fort had access to quite a few original Snider-Enfield rifles at the time.

The British army of the 1860s was made up of several branches, artillery, engineers, and infantry. At Fort Henry the artillery and the infantry are interpreted.

## The Artillery

The Royal Regiment of Artillery was founded in 1722 and in 1867 was divided into three branches: horse artillery,

*Artillery NCO beside a 24-pounder carronade*

field artillery, and garrison artillery. Artillerymen wore deep blue uniforms with red facings, exactly the opposite of infantry regiments. This was the tradition for artillery dress. It was convenient that the deep blue also helped

hide the stains that gunners often got on their uniforms when working the guns.

In the 1860s the Royal Artillery (RA) maintained a fairly large presence in Kingston, particularly at their main barracks, stable, and depot known as the artillery park in the middle of town. In addition to the large presence in the city, a detachment from the brigade was posted to Fort Henry. The RA did not have enough men to completely man the guns of the fort. The gunners posted there maintained the guns and taught the soldiers at the fort how to use them whenever possible. One can imagine that the infantry were not too keen on having to learn the ways of artillery. Generally, a gunner's life was somewhat better than that of an infantry private. The gunner was paid slightly more, his food and accommodation were better, there was more free time and less marching.

The Guard recreates the gunners' lives at Fort Henry and regularly demonstrates the loading and firing of the fort's 24-pounders on the east wall. The fort was primarily armed with these guns in 1867 so it is appropriate that the Guard demonstrates their use today. The drill and reproduction equipment are taken directly from the British artillery manuals in effect at the time. In addition, the Guard is trained in how to fire the fort's 24-pounder carronade on the east battery and also the two small reproduction 6-pounder rifled breech-loading Armstrong field guns.

Armstrong field guns were introduced into service in 1859 and constituted a revolutionary advance in weapons technology for the British. The new guns could be loaded

*Drummers*

## The Infantry

Originally the Guard was clothed in whatever Ronald Way could beg or borrow. The first Guard wore original 1880s era uniforms and equipment and carried the 1860s era Snider-Enfield rifle. Over time the Guard's uniforms and equipment evolved and Way settled on 1867 as the time period to be recreated at the fort. Continued research and refinement has brought the uniforms to the point they are today, as close to the British army of 1867 as possible.

The Fort Henry Guard represents a royal regiment of the line. As such, their uniforms are red with dark blue facings ("facings" refer to the collar and cuffs). There were several differ-

*A Victorian General Service medal*

ent kinds of facings worn by regiments in this period including various shades of blue, red, green, white, black, and yellow. These different colours indicated different regiments, but only those that had been honoured by the monarch were allowed to call themselves royal and have dark blue facings. Within the line infantry there were several

from the rear or breech, unlike previous guns, which had to be loaded from the front or muzzle. A breech-loading gun could be loaded and fired much faster than its muzzle-loading predecessor. In addition, the inside of the barrel or bore was not smooth but rifled with a series of long spirals ground out of the bore. These grooves spun the projectile as it was fired out of the barrel and made it fly farther with more accuracy and arrive at its target with greater impact than projectiles fired from smoothbore guns.

Today the Guard uses the 6-pounder Armstrong field guns regularly during battle tactics demonstrations as well as for ceremonial gun salutes. In addition, the Guard has annual competitions between gun detachments within the Guard itself and between the Guard and the United States Marine Corps.

*Bayonet drill in the parade square*

*Drilling the "The Thin Red Line"*

Balaklava in 1854 during the Crimean War. Most armies of the world fought with a line three or four men deep. The British, however, used a line only two men deep — and to great effect. It maximized firepower as it allowed every man to fire at once, thus delivering 600 to 1,000 rounds in one volley. It was a withering hail of lead indeed, particularly when compared to the 340 to 500 rounds other European armies could bring to bear using their formations. The Guard demonstrates the Thin Red Line regularly.

different kinds of regiments including highland (wearing kilts), rifle (wearing green uniforms), and light infantry (who acted as skirmishers in battle). By the 1860s light infantry were mostly dressed the same as line regiments.

Regiments were organized into battalions. Most regiments were made up of two battalions but some had as many as three. Each battalion was usually commanded by a Lieutenant-Colonel and comprised anywhere from 600 to 1,000 men (battalions were rarely at full strength, especially in wartime). Battalions were usually made up of eight to ten companies of 80 to 100 men each and split into two equal wings, each commanded by a Major, with a Captain being in charge of the company as a whole. The Captain usually had two subalterns, a Lieutenant and an Ensign, to assist him. In 1867 there were approximately 145 battalions in the British army.

The British army was famous for its "Thin Red Line," immortalised by the troops of the 93rd Argyll and Sutherland Highlanders standing fast during an attack by Russian cavalry at the Battle of

Another well-known formation is the "British Square." A battalion in line was an open invitation for cavalry to attack. The square was designed to protect the battalion from cavalry. Bayonets were fixed on the ends of the rifles and the men assembled around the officers and colours. The troops were four deep with the two front ranks kneeling and the two rear

*A fifer*

*A bugle*

In the nineteenth century, battles usually took place during the daylight hours in spring and summer, when ice, snow or mud did not hamper movements. Armies marched into battle facing each other, each trying to find the other's weakness. They fired against one another, often at point blank range, until one side was defeated. The soldiers did not fire unless instructed to do so. The British army was famous for its ability to withhold fire until the last possible moment. Finally the attack was pressed home with bayonets fixed on the ends of the soldiers' rifles. Casualties in this type of attack were usually high, but many more men died from infection of their wounds after the battle was over.

The Fort Henry Guard performs all these battle tactics, minus the casualties.

## Military Music

Most battalions of infantry had a musical group known as the Corps of Drums. Rifle regiments often had bugle bands under the direction of a Bugle Major while highland regiments had pipe bands under the direction of a Pipe Major. In a line regiment the Corps of Drums was made up of the twenty company duty musicians (one bugler and one drummer from each company) of the battalion under the direction of the Drum Major. The members of the Drums wore red tunics like the rest of the battalion, but their uniforms were also adorned with white drummers braid with red crowns along the seams.

ranks standing, all facing outwards with their bayonets pointed at the height of a horse's chest. No horse would willingly throw itself on this wall of steel. Since cavalry rarely carried firearms, the men in the square were relatively safe. One of the disadvantages of the square, however, was its vulnerability to artillery. Large clusters of men made excellent targets and a well-placed solid shot could crash through both sides of a square inflicting terrible damage. Exploding shot could be even more deadly.

Discipline and steadiness within the ranks were essential. In the 1860s men marched without swinging their arms and touched elbow to elbow. If a man fell in battle, the line closed up quickly to maintain a solid front. It was also important for the entire battalion to move at the same pace. If the line fractured at any point, the entire line became vulnerable to attack. When orders were issued to change the formation, the battalion was trained to react immediately since any hesitation might expose part of it to attack. This kind of response, and the often highly complicated manoeuvre required, was only achieved through many hours of hard drilling in peacetime. The Guard skilfully performs many of the intricate drill movements of the 1860s.

*Firing from a "British Square"*

*Drum and drummers*

fying that the final sentry had been posted and soldiers should be in their barracks with the lights out.

The Fort Henry Guard interprets a battalion Corps of Drums. All the music played by the Drums is from the 1867 period. Bugle calls are heard throughout the day just as they were when the British army garrisoned Fort Henry.

Most battalions also had a regimental band similar in composition to a modern day military band. The bandsmen wore white uniforms with facings appropriate to the regiment and were usually professional musicians paid by the officers. The band was at the beck and call of the officers of the regiment, particularly the commanding officer. They performed at various social functions throughout the year and were often seen performing in the town in which

These men were the battalion timekeepers and from Reveille in the morning to Lights Out in the evening, they played the various camp and duty calls necessary to regulate a soldier's day. Most soldiers were not wealthy enough to own a timepiece and there were not any clocks in barrack rooms. Consequently, drum and bugle calls were necessary.

Prior to the army's use of barracks, soldiers were often billeted in taverns and inns. In the evening the Drums would parade through the town, which was the signal for the innkeepers "turn off the taps" to stop serving the troops and for the soldiers to return to their billets. The Dutch expression for this is doe-den tap-toe, which the English eventually abbreviated to "tattoo." The ceremony of marching through the town evolved into a more elaborate parade that included lowering the flag, changing the guard, and posting sentries for the night. It usually ended with the bugle calls of "Last Post" and "Lights Out," signi-

the battalion was garrisoned. There are many examples of regiments, such as the 62nd Regiment of Foot, which garrisoned Kingston and Fort Henry in 1862–63, that had excellent regimental bands. The 62nd's band in particular played at various civic functions such as outdoor skating parties and theatrical events, as well as giving public performances of popular music of the day. The Guard does not interpret a military band.

*Drum Major*

*The Queen's and Regimental Colours of the Fort Henry Guard*

## The Colours

In 1867, as today, most regiments of the British army carried flags or Colours, which embodied the spirit and traditions of the battalion. The Colours were rallying points on the battlefield up until the 1880s, when they were no longer carried in battle. The Colours of the Fort Henry Guard consist of the Queen's Colour and the Regimental Colour. They are designed in accordance with regulations in effect in 1867 which stated that they were to be made of silk, to measure "3 feet 9 inches flying and 3 feet deep at the pike," and were to be carried on pikes 9 feet 10 inches in length.

The Royal or Queen's Colour was the "Great Union"

or Union Jack as we know it today, with the number of the regiment in the middle surmounted with the Imperial Crown. Since the Guard does not have a number, the letters FHG are used, representing Fort Henry Guard.

The Regimental Colour for royal regiments was dark blue and had the Union Jack in the upper left corner. The Colour normally bore the battle honours of a regiment. Since the Guard has no battle honours, its Regimental Colour bears the names of the 34 British and 28 Canadian units that garrisoned Kingston and Fort Henry during the fort's years of active service from 1812 to 1943. The Colour symbolizes the reason for the Guard's existence to remember those who served. The motto of the Guard is "We Also Serve."

*The Goat Major with David VIII on parade*

## The Mascot

The Guard carries on the British army tradition of regimental mascots with David VIII, a white Saanen goat. Many British regiments are known for their mascots. Perhaps the most famous is "Billy," the mascot of the 23rd Regiment of Foot, Royal Welch Fusiliers, who garrisoned Fort Henry from 1842–1843. To commemorate the services of this regiment, the St. David's Society of Toronto presented the Guard with its first mascot in 1953. Ever since that day, the Guard has always marched on parade proudly led by their mascot "David."

## The Pioneers

Every battalion in the British army had one pioneer per company. Pioneers were the skilled artisans of the regiment and they were recruited from the ranks from carpenters, masons, engine fitters, and the like. Interestingly, army regulations stipulated that pioneers had to be bearded. In the field, the pioneers usually supervised any major work that had to be done, including the construction of earthworks and defences. A pioneer's tools had to be carried with him and the regulations were quite specific about how many pick axes, broad axes, shovels, billhooks, crowbars, chisels, and so on were to be carried by each of the battalion's eleven pioneers. Today the Guard's pioneers parade daily for the public in the summer months.

## Regimental Affiliations

Over the years the Fort Henry Guard has been fortunate to work with many fine military and civilian groups. From the point of view of the Guard, however, their most cherished relationship is with the United States Marine Corps. Nothing stimulates the troops more than the knowledge that they will soon be parading with "The Marines." The Guard parades annually with the Battle Color Detachment of United States Marine Corps from Marine Barracks, Washington, D.C. Since 1954 when the Guard and the Marines first paraded together at Fort Henry, a unique bond of friendship has developed between the two units. From 1955 until 1990, the Guard's Honourary Commander was General Lemuel C. Shepherd Jr., a former Commandant of the Marine Corps and an avid military historian who was impressed with the Guard from the first time he saw them on parade. The Guard is one of the few civilian units permitted to parade on the Marine parade deck in Washington and the Marines are the only non-British or Canadian unit that have been entrusted with the keys to Fort Henry. As a sign of friendship, both units have exchanged ceremonial drums. Since 1969, the Guard and the Marines have paraded together annually either at the fort or in Washington, D.C. It has not escaped the Marines' attention that British troops once set fire to the home of the President of the United States, causing authorities to paint it white in the aftermath, thereby giving the house its distinctive name.

\* \* \*

Formed in 1938, the Fort Henry Guard has paraded every summer since 1948. Its purpose was and continues to be to breathe life into the old grey stones that constitute Fort Henry. Patterned after the British army in Canada in 1867, the Guard succeeds masterfully in its task of bringing the fort to life every day. Comprised of Canadian university and college students with no modern military affiliation, the Guard is known internationally for its historical accuracy, precision drill, and steadiness on the parade square. The Guard has performed twice at the prestigious Royal Tournament in England and for Her Majesty Queen Elizabeth II as well as for countless military and civilian dignitaries from many countries. As one can see, the Guard not only interprets history, it has made a bit of history of its own.

The following chapters will explore that history further, starting with Fort Henry's origins in the War of 1812.

*The Battle Color Detachment of the United States Marine Corps*

# 3

# THE CITADEL OF UPPER CANADA

## The First Blockhouse

The construction of the first fort on Point Henry was plagued by problems. The main difficulty was a shortage of building materials. There were too many ships to build in the Royal Navy Dockyard at Kingston and too many military barracks, blockhouses, commissariat stores, and civilian domiciles to be constructed in town for the wood and stone building materials available.

Kingston from Fort Henry, 1828, *by James Gray*

During the War of 1812, Kingston was transformed from a small transshipment point on Lake Ontario at the head of the St. Lawrence River to the linchpin in the defence network of Upper Canada. As Kingston was one of the critical links in the supply chain running from Great Britain to the western extremity of Upper Canada, the town's capture would have severed the chain and the upper province would quickly have been forced to succumb to the American invaders. As a result, it was necessary to fortify Kingston. While the first Fort Henry was very different from the one we see today in shape, design, and structure, its purpose was the same.

Naval Dockyard, Point Frederick, July 1815, *by Emeric Essex Vidal*

Although the British realized the significance of Kingston in the strategic defence of the dockyard and the town prior to the outbreak of the War of 1812, very little was done to fortify the garrison until after war was declared on 18 June 1812. The first defensive structure on Point Henry was a two-story wooden blockhouse built by the local militia between July and November 1812 when a report stated that "a blockhouse is built upon high ground for the protection of the harbour, mounting at present a six and nine pounder."

was concentrated on the defences of the town and the dockyard at Point Frederick. Only the trees to the west of the blockhouse had been felled.

*A model of the sloop* Royal George

## Kingston Attacked

Point Henry was witness to the first and only attack on Kingston during the War of 1812. On 10 November 1812, the small American fleet on Lake Ontario chased the Royal George, a sloop of war, into Kingston harbour. The ensuing battle between seven American warships and the sloop Royal George, supported by the artillery batteries on the Kingston shoreline, lasted approximately two hours. The 6- and 9-pounder guns atop Point Henry also took part in the fight. The Americans failed to inflict any real damage on the town and they failed to achieve their objective, the capture of the Royal George.

In January 1813, Lieutenant-Colonel Ralph H. Bruyeres, Commander of the Royal Engineers in North America, directed the blockhouse on Point Henry to be raised and improved. By April, however, not much had been done. Most of the work

## Fear of Invasion: May 1813

On 27 April 1813, an American force under the command of Major-General Henry Dearborn attacked and captured York (now Toronto), the capital of Upper Canada. The fall of York caused a general alarm to be raised in Kingston as the British were convinced that Kingston was the next target.

*The Canadian Voltigeurs in barracks*

Consequently, the town's defences continued to grow. In June 1813 Point Henry's armament boasted four small guns and 1,100 rounds of ammunition at the blockhouse. By this time the Point had been cleared of trees and the ground was littered with stumps, logs, and boulders of all sizes. One of the officers of the Canadian Voltigeurs assisting with the construction was Captain Jacques Viger of Montreal. His diary provides an insight into some of the hardships faced on Point Henry:

*Canadian Voltigeur*

*Broken down with fatigue, drenched with rain, I enter my tent to find that the birds of the air have besmirched me with lime; I have no sooner sat on my camp stool when a horrid toad springs to my lap in a most familiar way; I cast my wearied limbs on my couch, a slimy snake insists on sharing with me the folds of my blanket, I hastily retire and leave him in charge of my possessions.*

## Fear of Invasion: October 1813

Construction of the works at Point Henry continued through the summer and into October 1813. The American forces in the Niagara Peninsula had proceeded to Sacketts Harbour, the naval base across Lake Ontario from Fort Henry, to prepare to attack either Kingston or Montreal. From 6–15 October an alarm was raised as the town was gripped with the fear of another impending attack. The Americans felt Kingston was too well defended, however, and decided to move down the river in search of an easier target.

With the onset of the winter of 1813–14, construction at Point Henry was limited. However, one of the two stone towers to be built within the fort's walls was well underway by mid-January 1814. There was soon to be an extra burst of building activity at Point Henry as approvals had been given for the construction of a magazine, storehouse, carpenter's shop, and blacksmith's shop. These were all built in the ordnance and engineers yard located on the west side of Point Henry along Navy Bay, on the site of the present-day stockade, and were very much a part of both the first and second Fort Henry.

Throughout the building season of 1814, construction at Point Henry went forward with all possible haste; between 150 and 250 militiamen were employed there at any one time. By May 1814 the fort's stone walls and surrounding ditch were completed and some interior barracks constructed. By August 1814, the fort's arsenal had been strengthened to seventeen guns.

*H.M.S.* St. Lawrence

Fort Henry was nearly completed and very well armed on 10 September 1814 when H.M.S. *St. Lawrence*, boasting 112 guns, was launched. The *St. Lawrence* returned naval supremacy on Lake Ontario to the Royal Navy. Since the Americans were unlikely to attack Kingston without complete control of the lake, troops garrisoning it were diverted to other parts of Upper Canada.

Construction on Point Henry continued until the spring of 1815 when news reached Kingston of the war's end. Although the Treaty of Ghent, which concluded the war, was signed on Christmas Eve 1814, the news did not reach Upper Canada until March 1815. There had been rumours of a treaty prior to that date, but the fortification work at Kingston had continued. Now, work on the defences slowed but did not stop, as fears persisted that the treaty was only temporary. By 1816, the fort at Point Henry had been completed.

## "A good fort on Point Henry"

At war's end, Commodore Sir James Lucas Yeo, Britain's naval commander on the Great Lakes, summarized what had transpired:

*Officers of the Royal Engineers, 1846, by H. Martens*

*The experience of two years active service has served to convince me that tho' much has been done by the mutual exertions of both Services, we also owe as much if not more to the perverse stupidity of the Enemy; the Impolicy of their plans; the dissensions (sic) of their Commanders, and, lastly between them and their Minister of War.*

Although Yeo believed the Americans had performed poorly in the war, he and many other military and civil leaders in Britain were also convinced that another war with the United States was likely and that the Americans would not make the same mistakes twice. The most notable of these was the failure to cut off the British supply line into Upper Canada — the St. Lawrence River. If the Americans had managed to gain control of both sides of the river anywhere along its course from Montreal to Kingston, the British Army would have been forced to withdraw from Upper to Lower Canada.

What could Britain do to correct this transportation problem and not leave its Upper Canadian flank so exposed? This question saw all sorts of answers for the next thirty years. Regardless of the solution, Kingston — and particularly Fort Henry — always figured prominently.

Since the St. Lawrence was the main British supply line into Upper Canada, some alternate supply route was required. This alternate supply route would also have to be defended by a more sophisticated defence system. In 1819, a comprehensive document was prepared by the Master General of the Ordnance, the Duke of Wellington, which recommended the building of a canal from Kingston to a place on the Ottawa River (Bytown, later Ottawa). The document stated that "There must be a good fort on Point Henry." To put Wellington's plans into effect, a commission headed by Major General Sir James Carmichael-Smyth was instructed to prepare estimates and plans on the

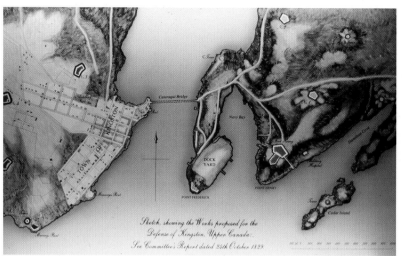

The plan of defensive works proposed for Kingston, 1829

construction of the Rideau Canal and new defences at Kingston. The commission submitted their report in September 1825 and recommended that £1.6 million (approximately $1 billion today) be spent on defensive works throughout Upper and Lower Canada.

In 1826 Lieutenant-Colonel John By, Royal Engineers, was put in charge of building the Rideau Canal and Lieutenant-Colonel Ross Wright, Royal Engineers, was put in charge of the construction of Fort Henry. By's massive overexpenditure on the Rideau Canal caused a new commission to be formed which changed the defensive plans for Kingston. In October 1829 the commission, led by Major General Sir Alexander Bryce, scrapped the extravagant 1825 plan and called for a circle of mutually supporting redoubts on the high ground and a line of towers and batteries for the water defences, all organized to protect the harbour, the entrance to the new canal, and particularly the naval dockyard at Point Frederick. Fort Henry was to be the largest of these, comprised of a redoubt for 300 men, with flanking ditches to command the eastern ridge overlooking the harbour and to protect the ordnance depot located there. In the rear was a sea battery linked to the redoubt by bombproof commissariat stores. The total cost for the "Citadel" was estimated to be £70,000.

Unfortunately, by the time money was allocated for Fort Henry, almost £700,000 had been spent on the Rideau Canal (only £169,000 had been budgeted by the canal's original surveyor). When the order to begin construction on Fort Henry finally came in 1832, cuts had to be made to the 1829 plan as a result of the Rideau over-expenditure.

The redoubts planned for Kingston were designed to protect each other with interlocking rings of fire. By the time construction began in June 1832, however, two of the redoubts and the fortifying of Tête du Pont Barracks beside the bridge in Kingston had been deleted in a further economizing move. The abolition of the redoubt directly to the north of Fort Henry led to the fort's modification from two to three fronts facing north. In addition, a caponiere was planned for the ditch to help with the close-in defence of the fort.

Construction began on the second Fort Henry on 18 June 1832. This coincided with the completion of the Rideau Canal. The first order of business was to dismantle the existing fort that had been built in haste during the War of 1812 and was in disrepair by 1832. Many of the Irish stonemasons who had been employed building the Rideau Canal moved to Kingston and found work at the new fort.

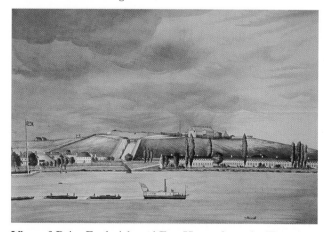

View of Point Frederick and Fort Henry from the Tête du Pont Barracks, 1839, *by Lt.-Col. H.F. Ainslie*

Over the course of the next five years, from 1832 to 1837, Fort Henry took its new shape. Lieutenant-Colonel Wright had been in Kingston since 1826 and had spent £11,567 quarrying stone at a number of local sites. He had not proceeded with construction because he had not been given permission to do so. Consequently, when permission was granted in 1832, Wright was ready to start. Plans were drawn up for a very modern fort that could withstand an attack with the smooth-bore weapons and technology that existed in 1832. Estimates for the project called for the excavation of over half a million cubic feet (14,150 cubic metres) of rock, for laying 150,000 cubic feet (4,245 cubic metres) of rubble masonry, for laying up over 100,000 square feet (92,900 square metres) of dressed stone, and using nearly two and a quarter million bricks to construct the vaulted bombproof casemates.

View South-east from Fort Henry, with the Military Hospital to the left, c. 1838, *by W.H. Bartlett*

The fort's offensive strength lay in its formidable guns on the ramparts. Perched 120 feet above Lake Ontario were five separate batteries of 24-pounders: on the east and west side there were batteries of four guns each, the northeast and northwest walls boasted six guns each, while the north battery had seven guns. The fort's eight-to twelve-foot-thick parapet (2.4 to 3.7 metres) protected the gunners. Each gun traversed in a 120 degree arc to sweep the glacis (the land surrounding a fortification and running up to it). To cover the branch ditches, the east and west batteries each included a 24-pounder carronade. In the ditch, the six counterscarp galleries facing south each held an 18-pounder carronade to cover the east and west ditches. There were also 302 loopholes from which defenders could fire into the ditch from inside the redoubt. In addition, the caponiere covered the north ditch in conjunction with the counterscarp galleries facing east and west. If the fort was besieged, there were under-

ground holding tanks replenished by rainwater that held 62,000 gallons (234,670 litres), enough for a garrison of over 300 men for 200 days, and 1,250 barrels of gunpowder could be stored in the magazine, enough for about 300 rounds per gun. There was even a way for the garrison to store rainwater to flush the privies. The engineers who designed the fort thought of everything.

Each room in the fort was an individual bombproof casemate with a vaulted ceiling made of eight layers of bricks. The bricks were covered with large flat stones, almost like shingles, a method of construction called "dos d'âne." The casemates were then covered over with several feet of masonry rubble or loose stone that was packed down tight to create the flat surface on the top called the ramparts. The resulting structure, while fairly bombproof, was not waterproof; throughout the fort's active service much time and money was devoted to trying to stop the inroads of water. Interestingly, in 1842 Fort Henry was one of the first places in North America where a recently invented substance known as asphalt was used. The asphalt was brought over from Britain, heated, and placed on Fort Henry's ramparts.

The main part of the fort, which included the redoubt and the advanced battery of nine 32-pounder guns, was completed by 1837. The filling and smoothing over of the glacis around the fort and work on the branch ditches took several more years. The Commissariat Stores and magazines connecting the battery with the redoubt were built in 1841–43 and the towers at the end of the branch ditches were built during the Oregon Boundary Crisis of 1846–48. The total cost of construction of Fort Henry, paid in full by the taxpayers of Great Britain, was £88,000, which is roughly $50,000,000 in today's currency. No small sum for a state of the art fortification in British North America in the mid 1800's.

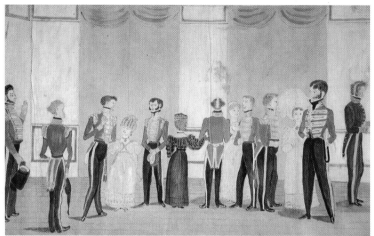

Regimental Entertainment at Kingston, Upper Canada, 1827;
*a contemporary watercolour showing actual officers from the garrison*

## Fort Henry Hospital

The Fort Henry hospital was situated in a secluded spot to the east of the fort near the shoreline and was surrounded by a wooden picket fence and protected by a stone guard-house. It was a two-storey limestone structure built by 1829 and able to accommodate up to twenty-five patients. It was completely self-contained, with a kitchen and latrine in the basement and a good well in the yard. The roof was made of tin, similar to that covering the buildings in the advanced battery. Following the abandonment of the fort in the 1890s, the hospital was gutted by fire. The walls were still standing in the early 1940s when the Canadian military tore them down.

## The Rebellions of 1837

In 1837 an insurrection began in British North America know as the Rebellions of Upper and Lower Canada. It was the start of protests that eventually led to the establishment of responsible government. Rebellion broke out first in Lower Canada in November 1837. At that time Sir Francis Bond Head, Lieutenant-Governor of Upper Canada, sent the British troops under his command to assist those stationed in Lower Canada. Bond Head was convinced, erroneously, that there was not going to be a rebellion in his province. Almost as soon as all the British troops had left Upper Canada, a small rebellion broke out north of Toronto. The militia was called out to put down the rebels and fear gripped the colony as more attacks were anticipated.

In Kingston, Major Richard Bonnycastle, Royal Engineers, was the senior British officer and he became responsible for defending the town from what was felt to be imminent attack. Bonnycastle and Lieutenant-Colonel Ross Wright had both been in Kingston for several years working on Fort Henry. When Wright left with most of the troops, Bonnycastle took over. He was well equipped for the task at hand and over the course of the next few months showed himself to be an extremely hard worker, well organized and up to the challenge at hand. Luckily, Bonnycastle was also a writer and his account of the rebellion time in Kingston is enlightening:

*The day was passed in reviewing, organizing, drilling, and disciplining the Militia, in ordering guns, bedding, cartridges, powders, flints and firelocks, in strengthening the batteries and Fort Henry, bringing old sandbags into use, which had rotted in oblivion of war. In mounting traversing platforms and drying the damp casemates, building ovens, and preparing safe places for the specie of the Commissariat and the Public Banks; in meeting the wishes of the rich inhabitants by providing bomb-proof vaults to put their plate and deeds in, and in arranging secure places in the event of the worst; in palisading, picketting, drawbridging, and, in short, in all the pomp and circumstance of war, with an infinity of its littleness.*

*Major Richard Bonnycastle*

Despite rumours to the contrary during the winter of 1837–38, the rebels did not attack Kingston. For his significant efforts in Kingston during the Rebellions, both in reinforcing the garrison's defences and in placating the frightened inhabitants, Bonnycastle was promoted to Lieutenant-Colonel and knighted.

## Aftermath of the Rebellions

In the midst of all this, a very happy event took place. The first child born in Fort Henry was christened on 4 May 1838. The young son of the fort's adjutant, Lieutenant Bates, was christened "Fort Henry Bates," and his father was given a sword, a sash, and £25. It seems Lieutenant Bates was held in very high regard by the militia troops that garrisoned the fort at the time and they stated in the letter that accompanied their gifts that they hoped "that the first born and scion of Fort Henry may never forget the circumstances under which he was born."

Following the rebellions, many men were tried and convicted of treason in Toronto for their participation in the uprising. Some were hanged, but most were sentenced to "Transportation." This meant that these men were to be sent by ship halfway around the world to the British penal colony of Van Dieman's Land, an island off the south

*John Montgomery*

coast of Australia known today as Tasmania. Quite a few of those sentenced in Toronto passed through Kingston and Fort Henry on their way to meet an oceangoing ship at Montreal or Quebec. Of these, there was a famous few that escaped from Fort Henry.

Montgomery's escape, as it became known, was named after the leader of the escapees. He was the owner of Montgomery's Tavern in Toronto, the place where the rebels met on the evening of their march on Toronto. John Montgomery himself always proclaimed his innocence and stated that he knew nothing of the meeting, or the rebel-

lion. History suggests that he was probably telling the truth, but he was found guilty along with many others. Because there were so many prisoners heading for Montreal, a very new Fort Henry was pressed into service as a jail. Because the fort's jail cells were not nearly large enough to hold the many prisoners, several casemates along the north wall were pressed into service. The one holding Montgomery and fourteen others was located in what is now the barracks room closest to the officers' kitchen and the entrance to the counterscarp galleries.

The prisoners were not interested in being transported and they were looking for a way to escape. They befriended the master mason, John Organ, and a casual labourer employed at the fort named Richard Davis. Both men proved invaluable in assisting with the escape. The wall connecting the prisoners' room with the room next door had only recently been bricked up, so the men began prying out the fresh mortar and pulling out the bricks. Work started on Tuesday, 23 July 1838, and by Saturday night a 2 1/2 foot square hole had been cut through the door. Once out into the next room, the escapees found the passage down to the counterscarp galleries that John Organ had told them about. They checked the route, found it was passable, and made plans to leave the next night.

Sunday evening, July 29, was an exceptionally stormy night according to Major Richard Bonnycastle's report on the escape. The prisoners got into the counterscarp galleries and then out into the ditch. They proceeded east but Montgomery managed to fall into one of the small drop ditches in the main ditch and break his leg. This slowed the group down a bit, but they pressed on in the driving rainstorm, secure in the knowledge the sentries could not see them. They continued through the main ditch to the east branch ditch and down to the water. Since the branch ditch towers had not yet been built, they were now free.

Several of the men were recaptured soon after the escape, but Montgomery and most of the others escaped to the United States. Montgomery lived in Rochester, New York, until 1843 when all the rebels were pardoned and he returned to Toronto and again opened a tavern.

The British authorities in Kingston were most upset when they heard of the escape. The commanding officer of the Kingston garrison, Colonel Dundas, hastily had Fort Henry's civilian jail keeper, John Ashley, arrested and held without a warrant. Eventually the real story behind the escape emerged and Ashley was released. Ashley was furious at being arrested and felt his reputation had been damaged. In an unprecedented move, he sued Colonel Dundas for false arrest and imprisonment. In an interesting court case that pitted a citizen of Upper Canada against the military and civil authorities of the colony, Ashley chose the young John A. Macdonald (Canada's eventual first prime minister) for his lawyer. Colonel Dundas, meanwhile, had the colony's Attorney-General, Charles Hagerman, for his legal counsel. In the end, the jury found Ashley's arrest justifiable. However, they held Dundas responsible for excessive detention, since the jailer was kept in jail for over eight hours without a proper warrant. Ashley was awarded damages of £200. The military and civil authorities were served notice that they were not above the law, even in times of upheaval.

*Sir John A. Macdonald*

## The Execution of Nils Von Schoultz

Another event of note that took place at Fort Henry just after it was built was the hanging of several men involved in the Battle of the Windmill. During the rebellions many Americans felt that Upper and Lower Canada would gladly join the United States. Some Americans formed so-called "Hunters Lodges" for the express purpose of attacking and "liberating" the Canadas. One such attack took place near Prescott, Upper Canada at Windmill Point from 10–16 November 1838 when a force of Americans, other foreigners, and some Canadian troops crossed the St. Lawrence from Ogdensburg, New York.

The attack was doomed from the start as the invaders were poorly led and organized. However, they did manage to occupy and defend a very well-built stone windmill that the British forces never succeeded in taking by force. The invaders surrendered on November 16 and were rounded up and taken to Fort Henry. The town was in an uproar when the 140 prisoners arrived by boat because there were rumours that the rebels had killed and mutilated the body of one of the British officers. The men were divided up into five casemates where they spent the next four to ten months.

The courts martial for the prisoners began on November 29. Nils Von Schoultz was the most senior officer captured and one of the first men tried. He also obtained the services of a lawyer, John A. Macdonald, who, although unable to assist in the military court, was able to give Von Schoultz some advice and did write up his final will. Von Schoultz pleaded guilty and stated that he knew nothing of the treatment of the officer who had been mutilated. He was nevertheless sentenced to hang, as were five others. Von Schoultz succeeded in capturing the imagination of the local populace. His noble bearing and his willingness to shoulder responsibility for an event that clearly was not his entire making impressed everyone. Von Schoultz tried to leave Macdonald something in his will, but Macdonald refused. On 8 December 1838 Nils Von Schoultz was hanged on the north glacis just outside Fort Henry's walls. Five other rebels were hanged there later on in the month.

## Oregon Boundary Dispute

Were it not for a political incident between Great Britain and the United States over the international border in western British North America, Kingston would probably be without her unofficial and most distinctive emblem, the Martello tower, and Fort Henry's branch ditches would have forever remained open to the water.

Britain and the United States differed over their boundary in the west. Britain advocated an area around the current border between Canada and the United States, the 49th parallel. The Americans were arguing for a boundary much further north at the 54th parallel. The boundary was particularly contentious in the area between Oregon and British Columbia. For a while, it looked as if the two countries might go to war over the matter.

As relations deteriorated between the two great powers, the people of Kingston began clamouring for the strengthening of defences in Kingston. The 1829 Smyth Commission had suggested Kingston be fortified with a series of mutually supporting redoubts on the high ground surrounding the town on both sides of the Cataraqui River. Since only Fort Henry had been built, more defences were needed. The British decided that Martello towers were the best and cheapest solution. In a move that was as much politically calculated as anything else, in order to appease the residents of Kingston and to be seen to be doing something to fortify the town, it was announced that four towers would be built. All the towers were built on the water. However,

*Canada 1858*
*The Royal Canadian Rifle Regiment ( Rfle, full-dress)*
*D.F.*

*Soldier of the Royal Canadian Rifle Regiment, 1858, by Derek FitzJames*

Kingston was still happy with the result. In addition, two smaller towers were constructed at Fort Henry at the bottom of each of the branch ditches.

Unfortunately for anyone attempting to build anything at the time, there was a great shortage of labourers and skilled craftsmen. In addition, those workers who could be had were asking and getting inflated wages. In 1846, the *Kingston Chronicle and Gazette* noted:

*With the certainty of an increase of wages from the number of men required and the rapidity with which the work is to be done with the chance of War, prudent persons have calculated on a contingency of at least 25 percent over the ordinary wages and costs of materials … However this may be, these works will cause a circulation during the next year of some 60 to 70,000 pounds, so that somebody will benefit by the expenditure.*

In spite of the labour shortages, the work got done and the towers were completed. Because war was not declared the towers were not armed with guns until the onset of the American Civil War in 1861. Happily for many soldiers both at Fort Henry and in Kingston, the towers became married quarters to deserving soldiers and a bit of a refuge from the grind and drudgery of daily barrack life.

The 1850s brought a more peaceful time to British North America as relations between Great Britain and the United States improved. Britain was involved in the Crimean War and troops were gradually withdrawn from Canada. By the late 1850s there were barely 300 troops left in Kingston.

*British infantry uniforms, c. 1867, by James Ferguson*

## The Royal Canadian Rifle Regiment

The one British regiment that garrisoned Fort Henry longer than any other was the Royal Canadian Rifle Regiment (RCRR). The regiment was formed in 1841 to combat the rampant desertion of British troops from posts close to the American border. Initially, to join the RCRR a soldier had to be of good character, be currently serving in one of the nineteen regiments in British North America, and have at least fifteen years experience in the army. The officers of the regiment were not required to have served a similar length of time in other regiments.

It was felt that soldiers with more seniority were less likely to desert from the border posts, particularly if they were permitted to be married on the strength. The RCRRs had a much higher percentage of married troops than the rest of the army and this, combined with their higher average age, did keep their desertion rate lower than that of other regiments. During the Civil War, American agents, called crimps, offered large bounties to British soldiers willing to desert and join the Union forces. They met with limited success among the RCRRs.

Like their counterparts in other regiments, the officers of the RCRRs liked to entertain their guests at the fort. On one such occasion, an Ensign Godfrey had the unfortunate experience of falling into the fort's ditch on a very dark night while assisting some ladies home from the fort. He later died from the effects of this incident.

As the number of British troops in British North America decreased during the 1850s, the RCRRs became the primary garrison in the Canadas. With the outbreak of the American Civil War, everything changed. Britain and the United States were on unfriendly terms during the war and it was felt that the Union forces might turn on British North America after they defeated the Confederacy. Battle-hardened British troops began arriving to reinforce Canada against possible American attack. This attack did not happen and the Americans dissolved their standing army rather quickly after the war.

During the Civil War, Fort Henry was nearly fully garrisoned with a complement of eleven officers and 269 men, down from the original 1837 numbers of eleven officers and 325 men due to military reforms over the years. In addition, the fort's defences were improved. The south curtain wall was raised about three feet (1 metre) and loopholed, several interior walls were taken down and rebuilt because they were in bad repair, and the east entrance to the advanced battery was completely bricked up to make the fort stronger defensively.

In addition, several of the rooms in the advanced battery were converted from storage rooms to powder magazines. During the conversion of one of the rooms, a workman was driving nails into the floorboards when an explosion took place that blew out onto the parade square. It turned out that the artillery had used the room for sifting gunpowder over the years and some had collected in the cracks between the boards. A spark from hammering the nail ignited the powder in the room. The workman was severely shaken by the explosion, but not significantly injured.

Although the Fenians, expatriate Irishmen living in the United States, did manage to attack Canada on several occasions following the Civil War, it was the Canadian militia that fought and eventually repelled them with the British regulars and RCRRs waiting as reserves. Fort Henry was not attacked during these raids.

On 1 April 1870 the formal disbanding of the RCRRs took place in front of a large crowd at the Tête du Pont Barracks in Kingston. It was a sad day for Kingston and Fort Henry as it signalled the end of an era: the last British troops were gone from the city. In the same year virtually all British troops were withdrawn from Canada.

## The School of Gunnery

A school of gunnery was founded at Fort Henry and the Quebec Citadel in 1871 by the Canadian government for the proper gunnery training for the Canadian militia. The schools of gunnery, designated "A" Battery in Kingston and "B" Battery in Quebec City, were a response to Canada's need to train its militia now that British troops had been withdrawn. The British had turned over all their fortifications and military stores to Canada when they pulled out, but much of the material was rather outdated. Weapons technology had significantly advanced with the implementation of rifled breech loading guns by the armies of the world. The fort had few of these types of weapons upon which to train; still, it did the best with what it had. As Lieutenant-Colonel Montizambert stated in 1885 "the guns and stores in this station are in good condition, but are, for the most part, obsolete. The gun carriages and traversing platforms at Fort Henry are more or less rotten." These schools of gunnery

became the Regiment of Canadian Artillery in 1885 and officially left Fort Henry in 1891.

The local militia regiment, the Princess of Wales' Own Rifles, garrisoned the fort during the North-West Rebellion of 1885. The regiment stayed from 1885 to 1887.

\* \* \*

Following the withdrawal of the artillery in 1891, the fort fell quickly into disrepair with the ravages of wind and water taking a heavy toll. Although a caretaker lived in the fort, he was unable to prevent the deterioration of the structure. What had once been the proud symbol of British military might in Canada was now reduced to a storage facility for the military. The fort had been at the centre of Kingston life through much of the nineteenth century and witnessed military trials, executions, prisoner escapes, and childbirth along with the drudgery and boredom of daily life in a garrison. Now all that was over and the fort, perched atop Point Henry, waited to see what events would transpire in the next century.

*British artillerymen drill with a 12-pounder Armstrong gun at Woolwich*

# 4

# FORT HENRY RESTORED

On 1 August 1938, Prime Minister William Lyon Mackenzie King opened the restored Fort Henry with these words:

*I declare this fort an historic site, not so much as Prime Minister, but in the name of those unknown British soldiers who laid the foundation of this land. I declare it open after one hundred years to further the cause of peace.*

The events and people who came together to bring about this large-scale restoration project are fascinating. Perhaps the most significant aspect of the restoration is the high degree of cooperation among the Federal government, specifically the Canadian Department of National Defence (DND), the Department of Labour, and the Ontario Ministry of Highways. Without their agreement to work together, Fort Henry would never have been restored. A second significant aspect of this was the drive, determination, and skill of Ronald Way, the Director of Restoration and Fort Henry's Director until 1965.

*Sentry duty*

## The Deterioration of Fort Henry

With the withdrawal of the British Forces from Canada in 1870, the fort gradually deteriorated as less and less money was spent on its upkeep. By the 1890s, the curtain wall was taken down for safety reasons. A more ignominious ending for a fort cannot be imagined.

In the early twentieth century, the fort continued to deteriorate, even though it was used as an internment camp during the First World War. By the late 1920s its condition was deplorable. The site was dangerous, rocks and stones were strewn everywhere, and walls were coming down. Many people believed it to be irreparable. While the Canadian military officers in charge of the Kingston district were aware that Fort Henry was literally falling down, their superiors were unwilling to allocate money to repair the structure. Local leaders also tried the more political route to get funds to repair the fort, but to no avail. In 1933 Anthony Adamson of the Architectural Conservancy of Ontario put together an excellent written and photographic report

*Reconstruction; Ronald Way is on the left*

on the poor state of Fort Henry. He presented it to the top soldier in Canada, Major-General A.G.L. McNaughton, Chief of the General Staff. The General was unmoved. Political events, however, were about to eclipse whatever the military thought.

On 10 September 1935 an historic meeting took place in Ottawa between the DND and the Ontario government. The new Chief of the General Staff, Major-General Ashton, met with Robert M. Smith, the Ontario Deputy Minister of Highways. The fact that the two parties were meeting to specifically discuss the restoration of Fort Henry marked a first in federal-provincial relations concerning historic sites.

Smith was the right hand man of his energetic minister, Thomas B. McQueston. As Minister of Highways, McQueston was very interested in promoting tourism, and he saw the restoration of historic sites such as Fort Henry, Fort George, and Fort Erie as a means to that end. During the meeting Smith stated the Department of Highways was greatly interested in the preservation and renovation of historic sites in Ontario, and that his present visit had particular reference to Fort Henry at Kingston. He asked if

the DND could repair Fort Henry sufficiently to permit it being opened to tourist traffic. He suggested that a long-term program of repairs be worked out and that "the Province might consider collaborating with the federal government in the work." Ashton replied that repairing the fort was a large task. He thought funds for such a project would have to be provided by the Department of the Interior. He sympathized with idea of "preserving and beautifying historic sites and promised to give the matter of Fort Henry full consideration, with a view of getting some action if at all possible." There appears to have been some precedent for the DND spending money on restoring historic structures since that department was presently repairing the old walls in Quebec City. At the conclusion of the meeting both sides emphasized their desire to cooperate as fully as possible.

Kingstonians began to take a keen interest in the fort as well. Stewart Lavell published an article in the November 1935 *Canadian Military Gazette* entitled "Is Fort Henry Worth Saving?" He concluded that it most certainly was but he stated that after 100 years, the fort was losing the battle with its only successful enemy, "indifference and neglect."

In May 1936, Norman Rogers, Member of Parliament for Kingston, Federal

*Ronald Way*

*Rebuilding the main ditch*

Minister of Labour, and a close friend of Prime Minister William Lyon Mackenzie King, forecast the restoration of Fort Henry, with the work being contingent on an agreement with the Ontario government. The federal and provincial governments were "much interested in the historic rebuilding of Fort Henry," according to the *Kingston Whig Standard* but there was no definite commitment to details in the article. Two days later McQueston expressed "sympathy with and interest in the reconstruction" and stated that he saw the fort as a "drawing card of high value in the tourist trade." An editorial in the same issue noted that the federal government was sympathetic to supporting the cost of restoration but felt it could not justify the high sums. This marked the first public disclosure of negotiations that had been taking place between the Ontario and federal governments for over a year. From the beginning, the importance of a restored fort as a tourist attraction was always part of official thinking and planning. Many felt that the fort could run at a profit, or at the very least, break even.

## Restoration Begins

By mid-June 1936 the federal government agreed to open Fort Henry for the period 1–8 August 1936, provided it could be made safe for visitors. Frid Construction of Hamilton was awarded the contract, for approximately $75,000, to complete the preliminary work on the fort. One of the peculiar aspects of Frid's terms was their request to borrow "four light railway dump cars stored at the Regional Depot, Kingston." These were horse-drawn and used throughout the Fort's restoration to move stone on a

*The first Fort Henry Guard on parade*

track that ran all the way around the ditch of the fort as well as inside it.

By all accounts, the fort's initial opening was a resounding success as some 7,000 people visited the site. The event sparked public interest and ensured that the restoration would go forward as a large-scale project.

Vision and a willingness to break new ground were both required for a collaboration between the federal and provincial governments to work. There was also a fair bit of negotiation regarding the terms of the agreement, both monetary and geographical. Since the province was interested in leasing the fort, Deputy Minister Smith wrote to DND on December 1936:

*I am writing to make application for a transfer by lease, or otherwise, of the property known as Fort William (sic) Henry, together with its approaches and including the martello tower on Cedar Island, the old hospital property, the two martello towers, connected with the Fort, and the martello tower in the harbour …*

After considerable negotiation, a deal was signed by Ontario and the federal government in April 1938. One of the sticking points of the agreement was the DND's insistence on continuing to use the casemates in the advanced battery as powder and ammunition magazines. Fortunately, a new magazine was built at the military camp at Petawawa, Ontario, and prior to the fort opening for visitors, all the ammunition was moved there.

Frid Construction Ltd. of Hamilton was again the successful bidder for the entire project. It seems more than coincidental that McQueston was the Member of Provincial Parliament for Hamilton, and known to be a man who looked after the needs of his constituents. William Sommerville was the architect for the project. His connection with McQueston was that he had completed a number of projects in the Hamilton and Niagara areas for the Department of Highways and he had designed the McMaster University campus in Hamilton.

Frid tendered $72,288 for the fiscal year 1936–37 and $305,448 for 1937–38. The first year's money from the federal government came from the Unemployment Relief and Assistance Act of 1936 while the second year's came from the Unemployment and Agricultural Assistance Act of 1937.

The number of men working on the site varied in 1937–38 from 100 to 200. A breakdown for April 1938, when 191 men were employed, shows that 15 were Frid's key men, 40 were mechanics, and 136 were labourers.

Seventy-five were hired from "relief" and 63 from "non-relief." Frid brought 15 foremen, bookkeepers and key men with him, but all the rest were hired locally. By the terms of the agreement, Frid was allowed to employ 25 per cent of the men himself. Frid employed all the stone-cutters in the Kingston area at the quarry near Barriefield and then hired from outside the area when the local supply was not enough.

There are a number of instances where men were hired for compassionate reasons. Those doing the hiring made it clear to their superiors that these men were in desperate need of a job. This is not surprising considering the times.

In total the federal government spent $400,698 on the restoration of Fort Henry while the province of Ontario contributed $426,994, for a grand total of $827,692. This included $27,178 for the paving of the road leading up the hill to the fort. The majority of the money was spent in the 1937–38 fiscal year when $481,468 was allocated to Fort Henry.

The whole project was not without its political bickering. R.B. Bennett, Leader of the Opposition, laid a number of charges concerning patronage against Rogers and those handling the letting of contracts and hiring of workers. Bennett's charges were all poorly researched and largely ill-founded. Rogers easily turned them aside during the debates.

## The Prime Minister Opens Fort Henry to the Public

Finally, after a Herculean effort to get Fort Henry ready, opening day dawned on Monday, 1 August 1938. It was cloudy and raining heavily, an inauspicious beginning for a day so important and historic. The weather improved as

*Coat of Arms above the main gate*

the day progressed, however, and the ceremonies took place as scheduled.

Ronald Way escorted Mackenzie King into the fort. King was challenged at the gate by the sentry who called "Halt! Who comes there?" He answered "The Prime Minister of Canada." With this the drawbridge was lowered and the official party entered the fort. The party included King, Norman Rogers, Colin Campbell (Ontario Minister of Public Works), and Brigadier Hertzberg, District Officer Commanding, Military District Number 3, representing the Minister of National Defence. King reviewed the first Fort Henry Guard, as well as a guard of honour made up of war veterans. A crowd of over 5,000 witnessed the occasion. Unfortunately there were very high winds and King tells us in his diary that public speaking was very difficult. Because the Ontario Premier Mitchell Hepburn did not get along with Mackenzie King, he did not attend and he strongly suggested that McQueston stay away as well, which he did.

The first part of the ceremony consisted of a formal transfer of the operation of the property from the federal government to the province. Following a speech by Rogers, King made the keynote address. The whole event was carried live on CBC national radio. Following the speeches the Fort Henry Guard paraded for the first time and demonstrated the drill of the British army of the nineteenth century.

The Fort Henry Guard has endured more successfully than Ronald Way ever imagined from that opening day. The original Guard was Way's idea to breathe life into the

*The Fort Henry Guard today*

"Old Stones." His innovative and trend-setting move was ahead of its time. Today, when every major historic site must have costumed staff or animators to exist as a viable attraction, it is easy to forget that Fort Henry was the first museum in Canada to attempt that kind of interpretation.

King was deeply moved by the opening ceremonies, as he knew that his grandfather, a Serjeant in the Royal Artillery, had been garrisoned in the fort during the rebellions of 1837–38. His mother's father, William Lyon Mackenzie, had been one of the leaders of the rebellion in Upper Canada. King wrote, "The visit to Fort Henry

King was very impressed with Ronald Way and he wrote Way a personal note of thanks not long after his visit.

\* \* \*

The reconstruction of Fort Henry in 1936–38 was a precedent-setting event in the area of federal-provincial relations and heritage conservation. It marked the first time the two governments agreed to work together in the field of historic preservation. They chose a huge project to begin with. The restoration was not without its problems,

*Opening day: W.Y. Mills, chairman of the opening ceremonies, Norman Rogers, M.P. for Kingston, Prime Minister Mackenzie King, and Ronald Way enter the fort*

itself was of exceptional interest. Indeed I shall recall it always as one of the greatest and most significant events of my life." During his morning tour of the fort with Ronald Way, King commented that he could be standing on the very boards and in the very room in which his grandfather had once stood.

given the immense scope of the work and the short time frame given for completion. That the project was completed at all is primarily a testament to Ronald Way and his singular drive, vision and energy. In addition, the Deputy Minister of Highways, Robert M. Smith, must also be commended for his work.

# 5

# FORT HENRY AND THE WORLD WARS

Fort Henry's massive limestone walls were built to prevent the enemy from capturing the fort. There were several times during the fort's history when these same walls were used instead to keep people in, particularly in the twentieth century. People living in Canada were initially placed in the fort as "enemy aliens" in the First World War, while German merchant seaman and soldiers were kept as prisoners in the Second World War.

## The First World War

When war broke out in Europe in 1914, the Government of Canada passed an order in council calling for the registration and possible internment of "enemy aliens." Many recent immigrants were now classified as enemy aliens because of their nationality. Austrians, Germans, and Turks figured prominently, although among them there were also some Ukrainians and other former citizens of the Austro-Hungarian Empire, misidentified as Austrians. The government was very liberal in its application of the alien term and as a result, many people who posed absolutely no threat to Canada or the war effort and who were in fact, tremendous supporters of their new county, were rounded up and put in internment camps. Fort Henry was the first of twenty-four internment camps in Canada to hold these newly classified "enemy aliens." When the first prisoners arrived at the fort on

*First World War prisoners play soccer in the fort*

*Pleasure craft before the Martello tower on Cedar Island*

18 August 1914 they were immediately put to work repairing and making the fort more liveable. It was in a deplorable state. By 7 December 1914 there were approximately 500 prisoners resident. Among these were teachers, professors, musicians, and people of many talents. In order to alleviate some of the boredom, instructional classes and lessons were set up using the abilities of those in the camp.

While there were a number of escapes and attempted escapes, one is of particular interest. The Camp Commandant had a motorized yacht that he kept at the dock in Navy Bay next to the fort. One day, the boat's engine was not working very well, so three prisoners (who were mechanics) were asked to repair it. The men did some work on the boat and took it out for a small circle of the bay to check it out. When they returned they stated that a bit more work needed to be done, after which they took the boat for a slightly longer trip. More "work" was then required and, following that, they took the boat for yet another trip. This time they did not come back and they made their way to Wolfe Island near Kingston. They were recaptured and returned to the fort soon after. Nevertheless, they had enjoyed a ride on the waters around Kingston in the Commandant's yacht.

Fort Henry was far from an ideal place for prisoners and soon after the war began, the Canadian government began building rural camps in virtually every province of Canada. Fort Henry Internment Camp was closed in May 1917 just after all the internees were moved to the camp at Kapuskasing in northern Ontario. The fort once again languished in a state of disrepair and continued to fall victim to the ravages of wind, rain, ice, and snow. There is a plaque to commemorate the Ukrainian internment experience in the fort on the south curtain wall.

*Objects made by POWs*

*The advanced battery from Point Frederick*

## The Second World War

When war threatened Europe in the summer of 1939, Ronald Way, Director of Fort Henry, began to hear rumours that the fort was to be used as a prisoner of war (POW) camp. Just after Canada declared war on 3 September 1939, Way was given one week to move the fort's artifacts and exhibits into storage. Way was not happy with the idea, but had no choice since the Department of National Defence owned Fort Henry. On September 7 it was announced that the fort was to be used as POW Camp 31 and just four days later the first civilian internees arrived by bus from Montreal. These internees stayed in the advanced battery and it is said they assisted with emptying the fort of its exhibits.

For the first few months the guards from the local Princess of Wales' Own Rifles (PWOR) lived in the redoubt and the prisoners lived in the former Commissariat casemates in the advanced battery. This changed in 29 June 1940, when 600 enemy merchant seamen (EMS) were brought to Kingston by train. They arrived at night and were marched up to the fort from the Kingston train station. The EMS were housed in thirty casemates in the redoubt, twenty men to a casemate, while the guards lived in the advanced battery. They had been taken off German merchant ships; many of them were barely eighteen years of age. In August when the Veterans Guard of Canada was finally formed, its members, mostly First World War veterans, took up their posts at the fort — and elsewhere in Canada.

There were many escape attempts during the three years the fort was a POW camp. One in particular was successful; most just provided some diversion for prisoners and guards alike. The POW population fluctuated anywhere between 200 and 400 men. At times all the POWs were enemy merchant seaman, at other times they were all from Germany's armed forces, and sometimes the population was mixed. When this was the case, there were often disagreements and fights among the prisoners since the two groups did not get along.

There were few actual escapes from Camp 31 and all escapees were eventually recaptured. However, there were many attempts and many instances of escapes in the works that were discovered before they could be carried out. On 21 March 1941 two officers, Gohlke and Rottmann, escaped through an enlarged loophole. They managed to cross over the ice on the St. Lawrence River to upstate New York, but were charged with illegal entry and returned to Canadian authorities (the United States had not yet entered the war). What's fascinating about the escape is the way Gohlke and Rottmann managed to get out of the fort. Over the course of the winter they had been throwing boiling water on the limestone rock that formed the loophole in their casemate. The water seeped into the limestone and the cold weather froze the water. The ice in the stone made it brittle and easy to chip away. Over time, they chipped

*Prisoners from the Second World War in the parade square*

*Prisoner's clothing, showing distinctive red dot*

away at the stone and enlarged the loophole but when it came time to escape the hole was not quite large enough and the men had to grease their bodies so they could fit through it. The board of inquiry into the escape examined the hole and refused to believe it was large enough for any man to crawl through. They determined that the men must have escaped some other way.

On 19 November 1941 Lieutenant H. Strehl escaped from the fort in a piano. The prisoners had rented two upright pianos from the Lindsay Piano Company in Kingston for some entertainment. Prior to loading the first piano onto the truck to return it, Strehl crawled into the piano. One assumes that Strehl was not a very large man. Once the piano was placed on the loading dock at Lindsay's, Strehl waited until everything was quiet and then crawled out. He made some noise and a female employee of Lindsay's came to check it out. Finding herself face to

face with a German POW, she screamed and ran inside to call the police. The police called the camp commandant, who dispatched some soldiers to pick up Strehl. In his distinctive blue denim shirt and trousers, with a wide red stripe down the leg and a large red dot on the back of the shirt, he was not hard to find. The commandant also checked on the second piano, still waiting to be returned, and found a second officer hidden inside.

Perhaps the most famous escape from Fort Henry during the Second World War took place on 26 August 1943. As noted above, the fort was built with an elaborate privy system that included a two-foot square stone and brick drainage "pipe" that ran from the fort, underground, down the west glacis to the water where it emptied its contents into Navy Bay. The historic privies were boarded up and off limits to the POWs. However, the prisoners managed to find out about the privy system and prepared to escape through it.

On the night of August 26, nineteen of the smallest German officers in the camp made their escape out through the privy system. When news of the escape reached the public the next day, Kingston was in a frenzy. The thought of German POWs running loose alarmed local townsfolk. Huge headlines appeared in the *Kingston Whig Standard* with photographs of some of the escaped men. Most of the men were picked up the next day. Many were simply walking around downtown, happy for a bit of time away from the fort and its boring gray walls. Others were a bit more industrious and the last one was captured some fifteen miles away by boat, in Clayton, New York on 1 September 1943.

*Second World War prisoners*

It was not long after this that Fort Henry was closed as an internment camp. The Geneva Convention expressly forbade countries from using fortifications as POW camps. While Canada claimed that Fort Henry was no longer a viable fortress, the Germans were not impressed and many POWs complained about the fort's damp and cold living conditions. The Canadian government had been preparing new camps in some of Canada's more remote areas in northern Ontario and the west, so it was not surprising when Camp 31 closed soon after its prisoners were moved to a camp in Monteith, Ontario.

Many former POWs have returned to Fort Henry historic site over the years as tourists. From interviews with these men it is clear that they were well treated while at the fort. Most of them talk about the incredible boredom they experienced while in captivity and how the fort's gray walls added to this. In hindsight, many realized how fortunate they were to have been captured early on in the war and consequently, to have survived. Some emigrated to Canada following the war.

The internment story does not end here, however, as the fort was subsequently used as a jail for Canadian servicemen under sentence. In April 1945, the fort was designated as Number 89 Detention Barracks and by May of that year 149 Canadian soldiers under sentence were being kept in the fort. There was a small riot on 14 August 1945, Victory over Japan Day — ninety soldiers had to be sent in to use tear gas and quell the riot. The fort was used in this fashion until the summer of 1946.

\* \* \*

The history of using Fort Henry as a jail is a long one. Almost before the mortar had dried on the fort's great limestone blocks, prisoners of the Crown were being crowded into freshly built casemates to wait for transportation to Van Dieman's Land. In the twentieth century, a broken-down dilapidated fort was called on to house "enemy aliens" in the First World War. This was hardly one of the fort's brighter moments. By the Second World War, a freshly restored Fort Henry provided what the prisoners themselves ultimately came to see as sanctuary from the ravages of that horrific conflict.

While it was initially built to keep people out, one can see that the fort was also quite successful at keeping prisoners in.

# AFTERWORD

Fort Henry was built to defend British interests from American aggression. In the grand plan, the fort and Kingston were meant to stop the Americans from gaining control of the important supply line along the Rideau Canal and the St. Lawrence River. By the 1860s westward American expansion had rendered Canada virtually indefensible along a border that extended for thousands of miles. Consequently, key fortifications like Fort Henry became obsolete and were left to languish.

By the late nineteenth and early twentieth centuries, the fort was in ruins. Through the efforts of a great many people a massive restoration took place in the 1930s which was the largest of its kind in Canada up until the 1960s. Both the Government of Ontario and the Government of Canada

*The mascot David before the redoubt*

saw fit to spend a total of nearly one million dollars to bring the fort back to its nineteenth century grandeur. Ronald Way realized the importance of bringing the fort to life for visitors so he introduced costumed interpreters, an innovative concept in the 1930s. Thus was born the Fort Henry Guard.

Since the 1930s the Guard and Fort Henry have become synonymous and millions of visitors have learned about Canada's history and been entertained at the same time.

Canada and the United States share the longest undefended border in the world. Once enemies, the two countries share a rich heritage that both nations' peoples could stand to learn more about. Let us hope that a visit to Fort Henry will increase everyone's enjoyment and understanding of our past.

# ACKNOWLEDGEMENTS

This book has been a long time coming. Having worked at Fort Henry in various capacities for nearly twenty-two years, I always wanted to write its history, but never seemed to have the time. I am grateful that a change in careers enabled me to complete this project.

I wish to thank the late Ronald Way and his wife "Taffy," without whom Fort Henry would not be what it is today. The Ways were an invincible team. I would like to thank my father Clarke, who first got me interested in Fort Henry and whose passion for history burns brighter than ever. I would also like to thank Diane Young and Ward McBurney, my editors at Lorimer, for shaping this book and bringing it to press.

Finally, I thank my wife Darlene for her patience and understanding through all the fort years.

*A composite photograph of Officers of the Royal Canadian Rifle Regiment from the 1860s*

# GLOSSARY OF MILITARY TERMS

**Accoutrements**: Articles carried by a soldier in the field, apart from his clothing and weapons.

**Advanced Battery**: A number of guns placed together under cover in front of a redoubt for its protection.

**Bastion**: A projection from a fortification, usually pentagon shaped, that allows those inside the work to defend themselves along their own walls or escarp.

**Battery**: A number of guns placed together for a particular purpose; also a platform where guns are placed within the fortification.

**Caponiere**: A casemated structure built to provide flanking fire to cover the ditch.

**Carronade**: A short artillery gun with a broad bore, often mounted on ships, and ideal for fighting at close quarters.

**Casemate**: A vaulted bombproof chamber built into the ramparts and provided with embrasures, gunports, or loopholes for defensive purposes.

**Counterscarp**: The outer wall of the ditch next to the glacis.

**Embrasure**: An opening made in the parapet or in the wall of the casemate for guns. Embrasures have widening angles from within for a sweeping effect.

**Escarp**: The wall immediately below the ramparts which forms the exterior wall of the fortification.

**Glacis**: The land surrounding the fortification. The glacis should slope up to the counterscarp and be completely clear of depressions or objects that would provide cover for the enemy.

**Loophole**: A narrow ,vertical opening, normally wider on the inside, through which one shoots.

**Martello Tower**: A round, self-contained fortification made of stone, often with a gun mounted on the roof. So named after Cape Mortella, in Corsica, where the first such tower was built.

**Parapet**: A wall of stone on the exterior side of the rampart built to protect troops and armament from enemy fire.

**Ramparts**: The area on top of the redoubt's casemates. It should be capable of resisting artillery fire and wide enough to allow the passage of troops.

**Redoubt**: A small, self-defensible, heavily constructed work without bastions or flanking protection. Its flanks are usually protected by other redoubts or through the use of counterscarp galleries and caponieres.

**Revetment**: A retaining wall of masonry supporting the face of the ramparts. They are the inside walls of the fort.

# LIST OF UNITS
# STATIONED AT FORT HENRY
# 1812–1943

| | |
|---|---|
| 1812–1870 | Royal Regiment of Artillery |
| 1812–1870 | Corps of Royal Engineers |
| 1812 | 10th Royal Veteran Battalion (disbanded in 1817) |
| 1813 | 104th Regiment of Foot (disbanded in 1817) |
| 1813 | Provincial Corps of Light Infantry (Canadian Voltigeurs) |
| 1813 | Regiment de Watteville (disbanded in 1816) |
| 1814 | Canadian Fencible Regiment (disbanded in 1816) |
| 1815 | 58th Regiment of Foot, later Northamptonshire Regiment |
| 1815–1817 | 70th Regiment of Foot, later East Surrey Regiment |
| 1817–1818 | 37th Regiment of Foot, later Royal Hampshire Regiment |
| 1818–1819 | 76th Regiment of Foot, later Duke of Wellington's Regiment |
| 1819–1821 | 70th Regiment of Foot, later East Surrey Regiment |
| 1821–1822 | 76th Regiment of Foot, later Duke of Wellington's Regiment |
| 1822–1823 | 68th Regiment of Foot, later Durham Light Infantry |
| 1823–1824 | 60th Regiment of Foot, later King's Royal Rifle Corps |
| 1824–1825 | 37th Regiment of Foot, later Royal Hampshire Regiment |
| 1825–1827 | 68th Regiment of Foot, later Durham Light Infantry |
| 1827–1828 | 15th Regiment of Foot, later East Yorkshire Regiment (The Duke of York's Own) |
| 1828–1829 | 71st Regiment of Foot, later Highland Light Infantry (City of Glasgow Regiment) |
| 1829–1831 | 79th Regiment of Foot, later Queen's Own Cameron Highlanders |
| 1831–1833 | 66th Regiment of Foot, later Royal Berkshire Regiment (Princess Charlotte of Wales') |
| 1833–1834 | 15th Regiment of Foot, later East Yorkshire Regiment |

| | |
|---|---|
| 1834–1835 | 66th Regiment of Foot, later Royal Berkshire Regiment |
| 1835–1837 | 24th Regiment of Foot, later South Wales Borderers |
| 1837–1838 | 1st Regiment of Frontenac Militia |
| 1838 | 71st Regiment of Foot, later Highland Light Infantry |
| 1838 | 73rd Regiment of Foot, later Black Watch (Royal Highland Regiment) |
| 1838 | 83rd Regiment of Foot, later Royal Ulster Rifles |
| 1838 | 35th Regiment of Foot, later King's Shropshire Light Infantry |
| 1838 | 93rd Regiment of Foot, later Argyll and Sutherland Highlanders |
| 1838–1839 | 8th Battalion of Incorporated Militia (disbanded in 1839) |
| 1839–1840 | 65th Regiment of Foot, later York and Lancaster Regiment |
| 1840–1841 | 34th Regiment of Foot, later Border Regiment |
| 1841–1842 | 43rd Regiment of Foot, later Oxfordshire and Buckinghamshire Light Infantry |
| 1842–1843 | 23rd Regiment of Foot, later Royal Welch Fusiliers |
| 1843–1844 | 93rd Regiment of Foot, later Argyll and Sutherland Highlanders |
| 1844–1844 | 82nd Regiment of Foot, later South Lancashire Regiment (The Prince of Wales' Volunteers) |
| 1846–1847 | 81st Regiment of Foot, later Loyal Regiment (North Lancashire) |
| 1847–1849 | Rifle Brigade later The Rifle Brigade (Princess Consort's Own) |
| 1849–1850 | 20th Regiment of Foot, later Lancashire Fusiliers |
| 1847–1849 | Rifle Brigade (Princess Consort's Own) |
| 1852–1853 | 91st Regiment of Foot, later Highland Light Infantry |
| 1853 | 54th Regiment of Foot, later Dorset Regiment |
| 1854–1856 | Royal Canadian Rifle Regiment (disbanded in 1870) |
| 1856–1857 | 9th Regiment of Foot, later Royal Norfolk Regiment |
| 1857–1862 | Royal Canadian Rifle Regiment (disbanded in 1870) |
| 1862–1863 | 62nd Regiment of Foot, later Wiltshire Regiment (Duke of Edinburgh's) |
| 1863–1870 | Royal Canadian Rifle Regiment (disbanded in 1870) |
| 1863–1864 | 47th Regiment of Foot, later Lancashire Regiment |
| 1870 | 60th Regiment of Foot, later King's Royal Rifle Corps |
| 1870 | 14th Battalion, The Princess of Wales' Own Rifles |
| 1871–1880 | "A" Battery of Garrison Artillery (School of Gunnery) |
| 1880–1883 | "B" Battery of Garrison Artillery (School of Gunnery) |
| 1883–1885 | Regiment of Canadian Artillery "B" Battery |
| 1885 | 14th Battalion, Princess of Wales' Own Rifles |
| 1885–1891 | Regiment of Canadian Artillery "A" Battery |
| 1887 | 14th Battalion, Princess of Wales' Own Rifles |
| 1914–1918 | Princess of Wales' Own Regiment |
| 1939–1940 | Princess of Wales' Own Regiment |
| 1940–1943 | Veterans Guard of Canada |

# HISTORICAL DOCUMENTS

## Introduction

What was it like to soldier at Fort Henry in the nineteenth century? Or to be a prisoner of war there in the twentieth? Why did Prime Minister Mackenzie King accord so much importance to the fort when he opened it to the public in 1938?

The following historical excerpts, taken from newspapers, diaries, and letters show how real people experienced Fort Henry in its heyday and its rebirth. In sourcing these, the author and publisher are particularly indebted to Arthur Britton Smith, MC, CD, QC, whose book *Kingston! Oh Kingston!* offers a complete compendium of writings about the city.

---

## Kingston Attacked

*On 10 November 1812, the American fleet on Lake Ontario chased the* Royal George, *a sloop of war, into Kingston harbour. The ensuing battle between seven American warships and the* Royal George, *supported by the artillery batteries on the Kingston shoreline, lasted approximately two hours. A week later, the* Kingston Gazette *carried this account.*

Early on Tuesday morning last information was conveyed to town that seven American vessels, full of men, were approaching. At day light the troops and militia were under arms, and detachments were immediately sent to occupy the different avenues to the town in order to give the enemy a proper reception should they be disposed to land. The Flying Artillery [horse artillery] were dispatched in advance of the troops. When they had passed Collin's Bay, several shots were fired by our Gun Boat at the nearest vessels, which they returned, but without effect on either side. At Everitt's Point one of our field pieces opened upon them, the shot from which appeared to strike several times, and they thought it prudent to steer further off. About two o'clock they approached the town and were fired at from all our Batteries. They opened and kept up a brisk fire in their turn upon the *Royal George* and upon our Batteries, which was continued till after sun set, when the enemy hauled their wind and anchored under the four mile Point, having done no other mischief than killing one man on board the *Royal George*. It is supposed that some damage was done to their largest vessel, the *Oneyda* [sic], as some of our shot from the Battery at Messisaugoe [sic] Point were seen to strike her ...

The alarm had been early communicated through the country, and persons of every age flocked into town from every quarter, eager to repulse the invaders from our peaceful shores. The veteran Loyalists who had manifested their zeal for their Sovereign during the American rebellion showed that age had not extinguished their ardor, and though many of them had passed that time of life when Military Service could not be legally required, they scorned exemption when their inveterate foes approached. Before night the town was crowded with brave men, who, insensible to fatigue, were anxious only to grapple with the enemy; who, had they attempted to land, would have paid dearly for their temerity.

*Kingston Gazette*, 17 November 1812

---

## An Eyewitness Account of Battle

*P.A. Finan was also present in Kingston during the November 1812 attack. He recollects a more varied response to the face of battle than was carried in the proud pages of the* Gazette. *He also records the shocking punishment meted out to deserters from the British army in time of war.*

Early on the morning of the 10th of November, 1812, the American fleet appeared in sight of the harbour, evidently for some hostile purpose. The military, militia, &c. were soon under arms, the batteries manned, and every arrangement made in order to give the enemy as warm a reception as possible. A detachment of infantry was sent to a bay about four miles above the town, where it was supposed they would land, and an immense degree of anxiety prevailed in town during the morning.

The approach of an enemy generally causes disorder and dismay among the female part of the community; and upon this occasion, when it was ascertained that the fleet was steering for the town, it was most distressing to see the numbers of women and children leaving their houses and hurrying in consternation backwards to the woods; some carrying bundles of what they most valued, others apparently quite satisfied to escape with life.

The *Royal George*, the largest of the only two frigates we had at the time, had been out cruising for some days, and about twelve o'clock it made its appearance, coming in from the lake with all sail set, and the whole American fleet, consisting of a brig of 22 guns and six schooners, in full chase of it. It anchored down the bay at the lower end of the town, and between two batteries, one at the upper end of the town on a small point of land jutting into the harbour, the other on the point of the peninsula opposite.

About two o'clock the enemy's squadron sailed down the harbour very boldly, apparently quite unaware of the two batteries just mentioned which had been lately erected, as they used no precaution to avoid them, but were bearing down, in full sail, upon the *Royal George* and firing with all their might. Our troops in the batteries observing this, allowed them to approach very near before they commenced firing, and when the brig and two or three of the schooners were just between them, they opened a tremendous and destructive fire upon them, in which they were joined by the *Royal George*. The Americans were evidently confounded at this, as they instantly put about; and, while in the act of tacking, the commander of one of the schooners was knocked overboard by the main boom and perished.

The batteries kept up such a galling fire upon the vessels that they were compelled to retire; and as the wind was blowing directly down the lake, they were under the necessity of beating out; whenever, therefore, they approached the side next the town, the batteries received them in fine style, and did them very considerable damage. The enemy did not fire upon the town, from which it appeared that their object was merely to capture or destroy the *Royal George*, as all their attention was directed towards it; and although they were obliged to relinquish the attempt they almost effected its destruction by a shot from a thirty-two pounder, which it received between wind and water, or half above and half below the level of the water.

We lost only one man upon the occasion, and he had been an invalid, confined to his hammock for some time previous, being a marine on board the frigate. When he heard the cannonading, he could stay in his hammock, but insisted on being carried upon deck; and his urgent request being complied with, he was seated near one of the guns, on the side next to the enemy, where he had remained but a few minutes when a cannon ball struck him on the side, and going in an oblique direction to the opposite shoulder, destroyed him in a moment, leaving his body a dreadful spectacle.

The enemy succeeded in reaching a small bay on the eastern shore, about four miles above the town, where they remained during the night, busily occupied in repairing as well as possible the damage they had sustained. On the following day they got under way, and while beating about, a

British merchant schooner, on its way from the upper country, hove in sight, making for the harbour; the crew, little expecting to meet an American squadron so near Kingston, found themselves almost surrounded by it before they were aware of their danger. The master, finding there was no chance of escape by attempting to return, determined, though to all appearance with but little prospect of success, to endeavour to make his way through it; he therefore made all sail, and, the vessel being an excellent sailor, and he perfectly acquainted with the navigation of the place, steered directly through the fleet, and although chased and fired at by all the vessels, he manoeuvred so well as to effect his escape, though not without receiving a shot between wind and water. When the schooner reached the uppermost wharf in the town, it was brought alongside the lower end of it, with the head towards the land, and, being full of water, it sank immediately, but luckily the water was not very deep at the spot. An immense number of people had collected at the upper part of the town while the vessel was among the enemy's fleet, to observe the result, and were at the wharf when it arrived. A strong hawser was therefore made fast to the bow of the vessel, and the other end being brought on shore, as many of the people as could get hold of it did so, and so great was the crowd that they actually drew it so near the shore that the upper parts appeared above the surface of the water.

Two of the American schooners not being able to beat up to lake Ontario, were obliged to sail down past Kingston, to Ogdensburg, where they remained until winter, when they were burnt by our forces at the capture of that place.

### "A melancholy and shocking scene"

One day, while taking a walk in the country, I met three armed soldiers escorting a deserter. As I passed the unfortunate man I glanced at him, and his eyes meeting mine, I fancied from their expression that I could read in them the momentary feelings of his mind; they seemed to me to say "Oh! that like you I were wandering wherever my fancy directed, unconcerned with respect to my superiors, free from guilt, and having nothing to fear!" This imagined

exclamation struck me very forcibly, and gave a thinking turn to my mind. "That poor man's countenance," thought I, "is expressive of misery; under his present circumstances he is debased to the lowest ebb of human degradation; poor, mean, despised; a fettered captive, marching with a quick pace to condign, impending punishment."

A few days afterwards the unhappy man was tried and condemned; and on the morning appointed for the execution, my youthful curiosity still panting for new objects led me to witness the tragical scene.

As we lived at the opposite part of the town from the barracks whence the procession moved to the place of execution, I proceeded to a street through which it must pass; and just as I reached it, the dead march, which the band was playing, broke in sad and solemn notes upon my ear; every hollow roll of the muffled drum seemed to warn the unhappy victim of his approaching dissolution; every concluding note of the parts of the piece appeared to measure his remaining moments, and to remind him that but a few more remained between it and his appearance in the august presence of his Maker.

I waited a few minutes until the procession came up, then accompanied it as it moved slowly on to the time of the dead march, whose lengthened notes appeared to sympathize with the sufferer, in being unwilling to hasten that awful moment, big with such important results to him.

The band led the way; the coffin, the gloomy cradle of death, borne on men's shoulders, followed next; and immediately behind it, pinioned, and guarded on either side by soldiers, the unfortunate victim to the offended laws of God, of honour, and of his country. The troops of the garrison, a long train, with measured steps and serious countenances, brought up the rear.

In a short time the procession reached the place of execution, a large common outside of the town. Here the troops were formed into three sides of a square; the coffin was placed in the centre, and the unfortunate culprit seated upon it, with his back towards the open side of the square. A bandage having tied over his eyes, a firing party consisting of six men advanced into the centre of the square, and stood a few paces in front of the sufferer. The adjutant then read his sentence aloud, after concluding which he made a few signs to the firing party, the last by a white handkerchief, being the awful signal to launch the fatal bullets at the prisoner. The unhappy man, on receiving their fire, gently fell on his left side, a lifeless corpse.

The troops were again formed into divisions, and, after marching close past the deceased, returned to their quarters.

As desertion was very frequent at this time, Indians were employed to intercept the deserters in the woods, and were allowed a reward for every soldier, dead or alive, they brought into town. One morning the barrack yard presented a melancholy and shocking scene. Three or four of the Glengarry regiment, who had been shot in the woods by the Indians, lay extended on the ground; one of them had received a ball in the breast while in the act of kneeling and aiming his musket; and his death had been so instantaneous that he became stiff in that position, his arms being extended and one knee bent; probably owing in a great measure to the intense frost that prevailed at the time, it being the depth of winter. One man of my father's regiment was found frozen to death at the foot of a small precipice, which, from the appearance of the snow on the side of it, he had frequently attempted to ascend, but had become overpowered by the frost before he could accomplish it. He was suspended during the day to the upper end of a long post, in a conspicuous situation, at the barracks; and the head of one of De Watteville's regiment, brought in at the same time, was placed upon the top of a long pole, in full view of his late comrades. This treatment of the dead bodies of the unfortunate men may, perhaps, appear very barbarous, and unbecoming a British army; but when the pernicious effects of desertion in time of war are taken into consideration, particularly at such a critical period as this was, as the Americans had become very successful in the upper part of the country, and the loss of the men being trifling when compared with the consequences that might result from the enemy being put in possession of the information that deserters might carry to them, the necessity of putting a stop to the baneful practice will be found to have tolerated every method that could have resorted to for that purpose.

P.A. Finan
*Journal of a Voyage to Quebec in the Year 1825, with Recollections of Canada, during the late American War in the years 1812–1813*
Newry, 1828

---

## A Young Officer Sees Kingston for the First Time

*Lieutenant John Le Couteur took part in the famous overland march of the 104th Regiment from Fredericton to Kingston in the winter of 1813. Le Couteur's journal provides a first-hand account of what it was like for a European to come upon Kingston, and Lake Ontario, for the first time.*

April 1813

When I reported the circumstances to Major Drummond [that the regiment, after arriving in Quebec, was to continue on to Kingston], who was marching at the head of the companies, one of the men exclaimed: "It's no wonder; they think we are like the children of Israel, we must march forty years before we halt!" Others hoped that, as it was the 1st of April, the General merely meant to make April fools of us, and let us off with a fright. But the 2nd of April undeceived us; we were off for Kingston.

I do not describe this part of our march from Quebec to Kingston, as many other regiments have performed it, none however in so short a space of time; it was nevertheless very severe, as the sun now had the power to thaw the snow and the ice over the small streams, some of which we were obliged to ford up to our middles, when the water was so intolerably cold, that the sudden shock to our pores, open from perspiration, was not a little trying to the best constitutions, and caused excessive pain in the loins.

On the 12th of April we were marching up a gentle ascent, and just as the head files were rising it, there was a general exclamation of "The sea, the sea — the ships, the ships!" The whole of us spontaneously broke and ran to witness the novel and interesting sight. Some of us had been marching between eight hundred and a thousand miles in six weeks, with only ten days' halt, during which time we had never lost sight of a forest, when suddenly there lay before our astonished and delighted view the town of Kingston, the magnificent Lake Ontario, and what was far more surprising still, a squadron of ships-of-war frozen on its bosom. It produced a striking and indescribable sensation, as none of us Europeans appeared to have reflected on the circumstance of being sure to find a fleet of men of war on a fresh water lake....

Donald E. Graves, editor
*Merry Hearts Make Light Days: The War of 1812 Journal of Lieutenant John Le Couteur, 104th Foot*
Ottawa: Carleton University Press, 1993

---

# A Monstrous Spider on Point Henry

*Captain Jacques Viger, of the Canadian Voltigeurs, was involved in building the first Fort Henry during the War of 1812. In his journal, he relates some of the hardships faced by his men while camping on and clearing the land, as well as an accident of war.*

The Voltigeurs' camp at Point Henry —
After having spent 21 days in the Barracks of Kingston, 10 days in quarters prepared by us, but not for us at a Mr Smith's, and 4 days in a camp made by us, but once more not for us, on the heights of Kingston, we were ordered by General Prevost on the 17th of May to cross over to Point Henry, where we now occupy tents which we again once more put up in a wilderness of stumps, fallen trees, boulders, and rocks of all sizes and shapes; sharing our blanket with reptiles of varied species; carrying out the precepts of the most self-sacrificing charity towards ten million insects and crawling abominations, the ones more voracious and disgusting then the others. Phlebotomized by the muskitoes [sic], cut and dissected by gnats, blistered by the sand flies, on the point of being eaten alive by the hungry wood rats as soon as they shall have disposed of our provisions. Pray for us! Pray for us! ye pious souls.

Broken down with fatigue, drenched with rain, I enter my tent to find that the birds of the air have besmirched me with lime; I have no sooner sat on my only camp stool when a horrid toad springs on to my lap in a most familiar way; I cast my wearied limbs on to my couch, a slimy snake insists on sharing with me the folds of my blanket, I hastily retire and leave him in possession. Let us have supper! The frying pan is produced to fry the ration pork. Horror! A monstrous spider has selected it for his web; he holds the fort in a viciously threatening attitude in the centre of its rays, he defiantly seems to say, remove me if you dare! The flinty biscuit must be pounded and broken or one can't eat it, here again the beastly wood-bug must needs crawl under the masher, and in losing his life infect everything with his sickening odor. Oh! Captain, what can we do? exclaims my valet. Fiat lux! What, Sir? Light the candle, you blockhead, light the candle. Let us write to our distant friends the excess of our misery. O ye gods, what a place this is! The candle is lighted, it is the next moment surrounded by myriads of flying things. My table is littered with writhing abominations, June bugs hasten from all sides, they besiege the light, extinguish it under one's very nose, strike you in the eye, and as a parting shot stun you with a blow on the forehead. What a paradise this spot would be for an entomologist!

We remained in this inferno a whole fortnight, but thank heavens these very unpleasant experiences came to an end and were followed by better times. After showing you the dark side of the medal it is but right you should now be shown the bright.

When we first came to Point Henry on the 17th of May, it was covered with stumps and the ground was nothing but holes and bumps. The trees had been cut down but quite recently. With much labour our Voltigeurs succeeded in levelling their camp ground. The camp consists of two rows of Marquises, facing one broad central avenue at the head of which are our Major's quarters and at the foot a small entrenchment. On a fine day our encampment presents quite a pretty sight. The Point is high and commands the view over all the surrounding country. We can here perceive the immense expanse of Lake Ontario, on the distant horizon a few wooded islands, to the right the town and its pretty background; the harbour and its sailing crafts; Point Frederick, its fortifications and shipyards are mapped before us; to the left is Wolfe Island with its extensive forests dotted here and there with new settlements. Away from the town and the control of the 'Big Heads,' under the immediate command of an officer who is popular, we can hope to live here in peace, quietness and happily ...

About the 29th of April I was officer on duty, and that night, about midnight, the alarm was sounded. I was then asleep in the guard-house. The news of the fall of York had just been sounded, and it was believed that Brother Jonathan was marching down towards Kingston. This news of the first success of the Americans during the war, made a deep impression on all, and many were the rumors that flew about. York, in itself, was not of supreme moment, but with it was lost an armed vessel and another about to be launched, with arms and supplies of all sorts for the troops farther to the front and in the west. A sudden call to arms is liable to cause a certain excitement and confusion, which led, on this occasion, to the death of our Voltigeurs, the first which has occurred since we have come here. At the first call, the men seized their muskets, and one of them, by mistake, picked up one which was not his own. It happened to be loaded with ball. He was tightening on the flint when it suddenly went off, and the charge lodged itself in the head of a young man named la Craubon, who died a few hours later.

Jacques Viger
*Reminiscences of the War of 1812–1814*
Kingston, 1895

---

## Letter from the Iron Duke

*Here are the Duke of Wellington's recommendations for fortifying Kingston in 1819.*

My Dear Lord —
I have perused with attention the dispatches from the Duke of Richmond upon the Defences of Canada, and the papers upon that subject sent to me from your Office, which I now return; and having given them every attention in my power, and endeavoured to make myself acquainted with the nature of the military operations which can be carried on in that Country — I am about to communicate to your Lordship my opinion upon the plans of Defence, for those Provinces.

I concur entirely with the Duke of Richmond that the Points of most importance in the two provinces are Quebec, Montreal and Kingston ...

The point of the greatest importance after Montreal is certainly Kingston. It is the connecting point between the Upper and Lower Province. It contains the Dockyard on Lake Ontario, and is the most populous Town in the Province, and at the same time so situated in relation to Sackett's Harbour as to be liable at all times to be attacked.

It must then be secured in some degree by Works, but without having more knowledge of the detail of the Ground, and of the positions of the several Islands than I can acquire from the descriptions and plans transmitted which I have perused and examined it is impossible for me to say what ought to be done.

As the attack must be made however by a combined Naval and Military operation, I would recommend the occupation with closed works, sufficiently armed, of Snake Island, and Garden Island. Those on the spot would best be able to determine how far this system ought to be carried, and whether there ought to be a work on Cataraqe [sic] Point and one on Simcoe Island. None of these Works need be very Capacious, or require more than 150 Men to Garrison them — but they must be well provided with Artillery of the largest description, and there must be a good Fort at Point Henry or elsewhere on the Mainland, as a Keep to these outworks.

Wellington to Goulburn, 1 March 1819

---

## Fort Henry in the Works

*These two remarkable eyewitness accounts, from 1833 and 1836 respectively, show how the Fort Henry we know today appeared under construction. The first account indicates the quantities of materials Fort Henry required; the second highlights the size of the fort as it was being completed.*

30 June 1833
A very warm day; took a walk to the bush in the forenoon, in the afternoon went across the bridge to

Points Frederick and Henry; saw a large quantity of cannon and cannon-ball and some very strong buildings intended for a Fort and Barrack. Saw the largest quantity of stone prepared for a building that I ever saw; it covered several acres of land. The stones were all marked, their length and depth; they were hard blue stone. The quantity of cannon and balls far exceeded aught I have ever seen.

W. Riddell
*Diary of a Voyage from Scotland to Canada in 1833*
Toronto, 1932

... a stupendous fortification of great strength: it covers an area of one acre; its walls and outworks are extremely massive. The fort and ditches are finished in an admirable manner, but it will occupy much time before the glacis is levelled and the outworks completed. The bulwarks and walls exhibit a formidable appearance. This gigantic work is being executed at the expense of the mother country.

Thomas Rolph
*A Brief Account, Together with Observations, Made during a visit in the West Indies, and a tour through the United States of America in parts of the years 1832–3; together with a statistical Account of Upper Canada*
Dundas, Upper Canada, 1836

---

## Surgeon Henry at Fort Henry

*Walter Henry, Surgeon of the 66th Regiment, was stationed at Fort Henry and Kingston in the mid-1830s. Whether writing about fishing, socializing, or the outbreaks of cholera in the town, Surgeon Henry's sharp eye and wit provide a vivid portrait of garrison life in early 19th century Canada.*

But we are now in sight of Fort Henry — presto — we are abreast of it. Anon the three deckers on the stocks, and the miserable remains of the *St. Lawrence* of 104 guns, make their appearance — we now round Point Frederick and the Dock Yard, and broad across the fine bay stretches a huge wooden bridge. Before us is the good Town of Kingston.

Kingston, finely situated on a rising ground at the north eastern and lower extremity of Lake Ontario, and at the upper end of the extraordinary Rideau Canal, is a town possessing great local advantages from this favourable position, and from the deep water of the harbour, which is sufficient for the largest ships. From these physical reasons — to say nothing of the strength of the military defences of Fort Henry, or the excellent character of its inhabitants, Kingston must always be a place of note; and by and by, when the wild land in the back Townships around it is brought into cultivation, the shores of the beautiful Bay of Quinte made the resort of emigrants, as they ought to be, and the impediments to the navigation of the Trent removed — this loyal and respectable town must participate largely in the general prosperity of the neighbourhood.

The bridge is a substantial wooden one, six hundred yards in length; spanning the neck of the Bay, with a draw-arch for craft passing up to the Rideau. The sail to the batch of locks, commands a prospect of finely wooded banks, of moderate elevation; and on each side patches of cultivated land and good farm houses appear in rich and luxuriant relief. This riant aspect is strongly contrasted with the gloom and melancholy of the view on entering the Canal. The black stumps of the half-burned trees sticking out of the drowned land — the solitude of the literally "dismal swamp" — the shallow, inky, and fetid water, with its unhealthy associations, are utterly disagreeable to the eye, and excite the most distasteful and unpleasing ideas: and it must be confessed that however advantageous to the Province this additional internal communication and artery of trade may be, the inundated shores of the Rideau add nothing to its beauty.

John Bull may have faults and weaknesses, but his generosity and kindness to his own family, admit of no dispute. He constructed this canal at an expence of a million and a quarter, at least, of sterling pounds, for the convenience of one of his youngest sons, who lived a great way off, and complained of being annoyed by the aggressions of a powerful neighbour. When the work was completed, John, honest man, thus addressed his child: "Now, my good boy, your wish is gratified — the canal is finished, I make you a present of it; only stipulating that myself and my servants many take a sail on it when we please, and that you and your people, for your own benefit, will keep the locks in order, and not permit a work to fall into decay on which I have laid out so much money." What ought to have been the answer of Master Canada Bull? Surely the most grateful thanks and immediate acquiescence. What was it only last year? "Much obliged to you Papa, but as you dug the canal you must keep it in order yourself — all I shall undertake will be to make use of it."

This has been for many years an Artillery Station. We found two companies quartered in a neat little barrack, clean and very comfortable; as that superior and most respectable arm of the service soon makes itself every where — with a snug cottage on a pretty eminence for the Commandant, and the officers' mess-house on the ridge above, commanding a glorious view of the lake and the bay from the windows.

Our regiment occupied three points here — the Tete du Pont Barracks, Fort Henry and Point Frederick. For the first month or two we were very healthy, but as the summer advanced the malaria from the Rideau swamps began to act on the men and we had a good deal of intermittent fever, generally of a mild description, and that yielded readily to medicine.

After a few weeks, when we had looked about us a little and reconnoitred our position, we began to bethink us that Lake Ontario was celebrated for its fish; and to take measures of hostility against the black bass, which we heard highly spoken of, as affording lively sport on the line and making a capital dish at table. So I bought a skiff, prepared minnow tackle, struck the top-gallants of my salmon-rods; and, one fine day in June, crossed over to Garden Island, sitting in the stern of my pretty little craft, whilst my servant plied a tiny pair of oars.

I had a rod and line at each side, at right angles with the skiff, and another line astern. Having attached a minnow and a gaudy fly to each, I commenced trolling along, with the stern line rolled up as far as was necessary, on a stick in my pocket. We had not gone a hundred yards when one reel spun away merrily, and there was a bass of a couple of pounds on the minnow-hook, leaping out of the water most

vivaciously. Before I had secured this gentleman I felt a tug at my pocket, and discovered that another about the same size was fast on the sternhook. I caught him also; and thus we went on, amusingly enough, for three or four hours; and returned in the evening with three dozen of good bass, a few of which were four pounds weight.

The bass is an excellent fish — firm, white and sweet at table, and very lively on the hook; leaping out of the water like a salmon. They are good either boiled or fried — at breakfast or dinner, and make an admirable curry. During our stay on the shores of Lake Ontario, I caught some thousands of them, and ate them constantly without satiety ...

As soon as it was known that malignant cholera had really appeared in Quebec, it was plain enough that it would find its way to the shores of Lake Ontario. My old friend, Colonel Nicol, was our Commandant at Kingston; and I well know what fearless energy might be expected from him in the midst of any epidemic, however deadly. We first had the barracks and hospitals most carefully cleaned and whitewashed: the duties and fatigues of the soldiers were lightened as much as possible, and they were daily inspected with great care by their medical officers. The canteen was placed under vigilant supervision, and preparations were made to isolate the barracks, and to remove the married soldiers resident in the town, with their families, to a camp on the other side of the bay.

On the morning of the 17th of June, a fatal case of undoubted cholera having occurred in the town, these precautions were carried into effect. A camp was formed on the hill near Fort Henry, and the barrack gates were shut.

Although the cholera raged in the town for the next fortnight, we had no case in the regiment till the 4th July, when two grenadiers were attacked with frightful spasms — I was sent for on the instant — bled them both largely, and they recovered. Ten other men of the regiment were taken ill, and treated in the same way: the agonizing cramps yielded to the early and copious bleeding, as to a charm, and they also all recovered.

Encouraged by the result of these, and several similar instances amongst the poor people of the town, I began vainly to imagine that his plan of treatment would be generally successful; and wrote confidently to this effect to Dr.

Skey: but I was soon to be undeceived. Three men and a woman, of the 66th, were attacked the same night. I saw them immediately; and the symptoms being the same to all appearance, they were bled like the others, and all died within twelve hours of the first attack. The spot which their barrack at Point Frederick occupied, was a promontory near the dock-yard, the air of which was vitiated by the neighbourhood of the rotting ships. The company quartered there was removed to camp on the hill the next morning, and had no more cholera ...

The appearance of Kingston during the epidemic was most melancholy ... Nothing was seen in the streets but these melancholy processions. No business was done, for the country people kept aloof from the infected town. The yellow flag was hoisted near the market place on the beach, and intercourse with the Steamboats put under Quarantine regulations. The conduct of the inhabitants was admirable, and reflected great credit on this good little town. The Medical men and the Clergy of all persuasions, vied with each other in the fearless discharge of their respective dangerous duties; and the exertions of all classes were judicious, manly and energetic: for the genuine English spirit shewed itself, as usual, undaunted in the midst of peril and rising above it.

We had thirty-six cases of bad cholera, besides a host of choleroid complaints, in the regiment. Of these we lost five men and two women. No child suffered.

During the prevalence of the disease it seemed to me that a number of errors in diet were generally entertained and acted on in our little community. Because unripe fruit, or excess in its use does mischief, all fruit was now proscribed by common opinion; and vegetables of every description were placed under the same ban, so that the gardeners saw their finest productions rotting unsaleable. This was folly; for the stomach was more likely to suffer than to benefit from the want of its accustomed pabulum of mixed animal and vegetable substances. It was proper to live temperately — to avoid supper eating, or eating late in the day — as eight-tenths of the attacks came on in the night — to eschew excesses of all kinds — but, above all to be fearless and place confidence in Providence.

If, amidst so much distress, ludicrous ideas could be entertained, there was enough to excite them on this sub-ject of abstinence from vegetables. Huge Irishmen who had sucked in the national root with their mother's milk, and lived on it all their lives, now shrank from a potato as poison. I heard a respectable and intelligent gentleman confess that he was tempted by the attractive appearance of a dish of green pease, and ate one pea, but he felt uncomfortable afterwards, and was sure it had disagreed with him.

The disease ceased entirely, and the usual intercourse was restored betwee the Garrison and the Town in the midst of October ...

Nothing strikes a stranger more than the mute solitude of the woods in Canada; for no sound, except the chirp of a squirrel or the croak of a frog, is ever heard in the interminable forest: and these but rarely. Even woodpeckers are found on the skirts of the woods only, close to cultivated ground, where the sun vivifies the insects on which they feed. Yet the cause is obvious — the severity of the winter drives away the feathered tribes, and the migrating races either remain in the cleared country during the summer, or retire to breed in the most secluded depths of the mountain forest, far away from the haunts of man. An oppressive feeling of melancholy comes over one in passing through the gloomy recesses of a Canadian forest; seeing at every step the decay of vegetable nature, bestriding the rotten trees, and perceiving the living ones half-choked by pressure and confinement, and contending with each other for air and sunshine. No gay creepers entwine their trunks — no flowers gem the ground at their roots — no turf covers the earth about them. All is cheerless, and unadorned, and monotonous gloom and silence.

In the young woods near the towns, the case is different. Animated life and abundance of wild flowers will here be met with, and the sportsman will find woodcocks and partridges in respectable numbers ...

Our regiment soon became popular at Kingston. We flattered ourselves that we were well conducted, and it is certain that the people were staunch in their British feelings, and well disposed and friendly to the military. Thus the main elements of kindly sentiments on both sides being in existence, it was easy bring to them into operation, and a degree of mutual attachment sprung up. We spent two years very pleasantly in our quiet quarters, partaking of much attention and hospitality. The first winter made us quite acquainted with our new friends and the second would have been still more agreeable, had it not been shaded a little by the recent ravages of the cholera ...

Warned by the experience of 1832, no time was lost in isolating the Garrison as much as possible. When the first case of malignant cholera took place in the town, the barrack gates were shut as formerly — the married soldiers living in lodgings with their families, were encamped near Fort Henry, on the same ground as before. The Royal Artillery having become sickly, were also sent to camp. These measures proved highly useful — the health of the numerous women and children was preserved, and that of the Artillery restored.

A strict hygeian police was established and sedulously maintained in the regiment, with the object of watching and crushing the first germ of the malady. Any deviation form the men's ordinary habits was at once noticed by steady non-commissioned officers appointed for this purpose, and reported to the surgeons. They were directed to observe the men at their meals carefully, and give notice if they should perceive loss of appetite in any individual. Drills and parades were discontinued, and all duties made as light as possible; but the men were marched a short distance in the cool of the evening by the Adjutant, after medical inspection. On hot days they were permitted to amuse themselves, and cool the barracks by watering them and the square in which they stood with a fire engine in which they enjoyed themselves much, making *jets d'eau* in the air *ad libitum*. Cleanliness of person, clothing, bedding and barrack rooms, was strictly enjoined and maintained. The men were allowed to take reasonable rest in the morning, and their sleep at that hour, which is generally the most refreshing after a hot night in a barrack room, was not abridged under a tenure little better than a day's, or even an hour's purchase. I went, therefore, on a visit to some friends residing on the Bay of Quinte, having been promised good snipe shooting in that quarter ...

1837 — The American friends of the Canadian insurgents were not idle in aid of their attempt, but their operations were confined to the Upper Province — no assistance of any consequence being afforded in the Lower. On the 12th of November a large party of armed men embarked in a schooner, and an American steamboat at Oswego, which took them down to Ogdensburg. Here they obtained possession of the boat and crossed over direct to Prescott; but finding opposition likely as they approached the wharf, they dropped down the river a couple of miles and then landed. These invaders, two hundred and fifty in number, under the command of a Pole named Von Schoultz, immediately occupied a strong stone windmill and some houses, and built breastwork on a commanding position for three guns they had brought with them: they then looked anxiously for reinforcements from the opposite side. But the activity of a couple of armed British steamboats, and of Colonel Worth of the American Army, prevented any aid from passing the river, and these daring brigands now found themselves cut off from the American shore — no individual joined them; but on the contrary the neighbouring militia assembled promptly to destroy them. They were attacked almost immediately with the greatest gallantry by a combined force of Militia, a detachment from the Royal Marines and another of the 83rd Regiment. The invaders were obliged to abandon their exterior defences and confine themselves to the windmill and a couple of stone houses, which they maintained with bravery and resolution. Finally, the militia were forced to retire from the attack; first planting a line of investing pickets — after sustaining a loss of about eighty men.

A very gallant officer of the 83rd, Lieutenant Johnston, and a brave militia officer, named Dalmage, here lost their lives, and the whole loss was much greater than yet sustained. The body of poor Johnston was shamefully and brutally mutilated.

It now became necessary to wait for the arrival of heavy Artillery from Kingston; and on the 15th November, Lieut. Colonel Dundas, commanding the 83rd, brought down a wing of his regiment and two eighteen pounders, whilst Captain Sandom, the Naval commander on the lakes, also brought some heavy guns. the result was the capture of the remaining invaders with scarcely any loss: one hundred and sixty-two of them were imprisoned at Fort Henry, near Kingston.

Walter Henry, Surgeon of the 66th Regiment
*Trifles from My Port-Folio*
Quebec, 1839

_____

# Rebellion Panic!

*This visitor to Kingston in the time of the Rebellions was a little amused at the extremes to which townspeople went to safeguard themselves in the event of an attack.*

Upon an eminence across the bay stands Fort Henry, which commands the approaches by the river, and also the town itself, in every direction. As a military station, Kingston is one of some importance, and by further artificial means might readily be converted into a very strong position, being in a great measure the key to Lake Ontario ...

I shall not easily forget the dismay which prevailed amongst the Kingstonians, when the news arrived that a body of from four hundred to five hundred marauders had encamped on Hickory Island, nearly opposite Gananoque, and were to march that night on Kingston, where they expected to be joined by a body of malcontents, from the heart of a partially disaffected township, a few miles off; and that, in the event of success crowning the undertaking, the town was to be given up to plunder, and every enormity committed.

Plate, money, jewels, and other valuables, together with the specie belonging to the local bank, were hastily collected, and dodged, for greater security, in the fort. A town-guard embodying every man capable of bearing arms (as far as the supply of the latter would admit), was hastily enrolled; the little garrison of the fort reinforced; the town barrack, wherein some militia were quartered, doubly guarded; and, in fine, every precaution taken that the shortness of time rendered practicable; succour being furthermore solicited from the environs.

As night approached, the general anxiety became very great, and anticipation was excited to the uttermost by the propagation of surmises and reports, regarding the progress of the enemy's movements.

Comparing small things with great, the scene and preparation might possibly have borne some analogy with what is represented to have taken place at Bruxelles [sic] on the eve of the battle of Waterloo, when the French were reported to be within a few hours' march.

To know friends from enemies in the confusion of a nocturnal conflict, the defenders of the town were enjoined to bind round their caps, as a badge of recognition, a strip of white linen. Candour compels to add, without the least disparagement to the valour of any, that in many cases the adornment appeared to be superfluous; since the paleness of the lengthened visages beneath it would have fairly borne the palm from the whitest linen that was ever bleached.

I know not how far this remark might have been exemplified in my own individuality, but I had at least a sort of right to look woe-begone, inasmuch as my only weapon of defence or offence was a half-rusty sabre, alike guiltless of edge, point, or sheath (I believe it had a handle), which was all I had been able to secure in the general scramble which took place for arms.

Perambulating the town in the course of the evening, I fell in with a gentleman of my acquaintance, who, armed to the teeth, was hurrying to his quarters to prepare, he said, for action, since positive information had just been received by the commandant, that the redoubted enemy was actually on his march, and would reach Kingston by eleven o'clock at the latest.

This was sufficiently precise, even for a non-alarmist, which I professed to be; so, leaving the streets to their solitude, I returned to my abode, there to await patiently the issue of events.

Eleven o'clock came, twelve, one, but still no enemy made his appearance, whereupon, becoming drowsy; I gave up watching, and regardless of what might happen, lay down to rest, though without disrobing, or parting with my trusty sword.

My readers will here naturally conclude that my repose was of short duration, and that I have yet in store for them the description of a stirring scene of strife. But no such thing. Unbroken were my slumbers throughout the night; and on awakening the next morning it was to learn, not that an attack had been made and foiled, but that the enemy had effectually belied the reports of the previous evening, by decamping from Hickory Island without even attempting an invasion of the mainland, on ascertaining the measures which had been taken to give him a warm reception, as well at Gananoque as at Kingston.

That mischief was averted by the show of preparation made, cannot reasonably be doubted; but it is no less certain that the means of aggression of the marauders had been greatly exaggerated, though it was satisfactorily established that they had confederates within the town, which had, furthermore, recently been entered by persons from the back country, under very suspicious circumstances.

It is probable that the enemy calculated on surprising and firing the town, with the view to plunder it; in which case, in the midst of the confusion, he might have succeeded in carrying off his booty. But he could have scarcely hoped to maintain himself in his position without first making himself master of Fort Henry, a task of no slight difficulty. It was, indeed, said that defection reigned among its garrison, consisting chiefly of militia; but this, appearing to rest rather on surmise than proof, obtained but little credit.

T.R. Preston
*Three Years Residence in Canada, 1837 to 1839*
London, 1840

---

## Lines Written at Fort Henry

*This poem was written by a volunteer in the Canadian militia during the rebellion crisis of 1837.*

If you think the following lines, scribbled whilst leaning on the carriage of a gun, worthy of a place in your columns, I shall be pleased to see them there.
— A Volunteer, First Lennox

High on Fort Henry's walls I stand
A glorious flag waves o'er me,
Beneath me spreads a bright, fair land,
The deep, broad lake before me.

St. Lawrence, with his thousand isles,
Rolls still and swiftly by,
And high above me brightly smiles
A clear and azure sky.

And round me, near are hearts and arms,
Nerv'd for their country's right,
Neglecting home and all its charms
Have rush'd, prepared for fight.

With panting hearts they long to meet
The recreant 'Yankee' foe,
Who, dead to every sense of shame,
Our State would overthrow.

But ne'er while yon proud Ensign waves
Upon the curling breeze
Shall bands of miscreant robber slaves,
Our rights and freedom seize.

No! Tho' home and friendship's ties are sweet,
Yet sweeter than them all,
At duty's summons, foes to meet,
OR DIE AT FREEDOM'S CALL!

---

## Escape from Fort Henry

*John Montgomery owned a tavern where William Lyon Mackenzie and his fellow Canadian rebels had gathered in December of 1837. Taken prisoner, Montgomery was awaiting trial in Fort Henry in July of 1838. He escaped, despite breaking his leg in the process, and went on to live in the United States until all the rebels were pardoned in 1843. The following is his own account.*

We had learned that a portion of the wall in our room, although four and a half feet thick, had been completed only a short time, and the mortar was not yet dry. Behind this wall was an oak door, leading to a subterranean passage which opened into a gun room; and as the shutters which covered the port holes hung on chains, we could easily let ourselves down by means of ropes made of our sheets into the sally port of a depth of ten feet; and by the same means were enabled to get on level ground. Our sole implements of labour consisted of a piece of iron ten inches in length, and a disk nail. Having obtained half a cord of wood, we piled it up in the middle of the floor, as if for the purpose of airing our bed-clothes, but in reality to hide the stone and mortar which we took from the hole ...

We, at length, went boldly to work; the unusual noise at first attracted the sentry, who came up to the window where I was reading the Bible, and asked the cause of it. I answered by pointing to two men, who, apparently for their amusement, but in reality to deaden the strokes on the wall, were, with shovel and tongs, beating the stove with all their might, and eliciting thereby roars of laughter from their companions: while I earnestly requested them to stop such trifling, and think of their apparently serious position ... We commenced on Tuesday and it was Sunday ere we had made a hole sufficiently large enough to enable us to go through. As the keeper had been married the Thursday before, we begged him to take his wife to church, and allow us to refrain from our usual airing. This he was very glad to do ...

When the guard beat the evening tattoo and descended from the ramparts, we commenced our escape. We reached the sally port in safety; but here I had the misfortune to fall into the pit and break my leg. One of my companions descended and took my hand, and we were pulled up by the rest ... It was a fearful night of storm and lightning, but we decided to take down towards the river, and when daylight came to take the woods. We had resolved to divide into parties for greater safety. We therefore divided our biscuits equally among fourteen men, Brophy Morden, Chase and myself decided to make for Cape Vincent agreeing to meet the others at Watertown, should we not be retaken.

from G.F.G. Stanley and R.A. Preston
*A Short History of Kingston as a Military and Naval Centre*
Kingston, 1950

# A Fearless Farewell

*Nils Von Schoultz was captured during the Battle of the Windmill, part of the 1837 Rebellion in Upper Canada. Although defended by John A. Macdonald (the future Prime Minister), Schoultz was found guilty and hanged at Fort Henry. His fearlessness and decency gained him the sympathy of Kingstonians.*

## Execution of Nils Von Schoultz

The Warrant for the execution of this person arrived in town on Wednesday night from the seat of Government addressed to the Sheriff of the Midland District. On Thursday the prisoner was removed from Fort Henry to the common goal and from thence at 8 o'clock this morning, he was taken to the glacis of Fort Henry and there hanged.

Final Letter
Kingston, December 7

When you get this letter I am no more. I have been informed that my execution will take place tomorrow. May God forgive them who brought me to this untimely death. I have made up my mind and I forgive them. Today I have been promised a lawyer to draw up my will. I have appointed you the executor of said will. I wrote to you in my former letter about my body. If the British Government permit it, I wish it may be delivered to you to be buried on your farm. I have no time to write to you because I have great need of communicating with my Creator and prepare for his Presence. The time has been very short that has been allowed. My last wish to the Americans is that they may not think of revenging my death: let no further blood be shed. And believe me, from what I have seen, that all the stories that were told about the sufferings of the Canadian people were untrue. Give my love to your sister and tell her I think on her as on my mother. God reward her for all her kindness. I further beg you to take care of W. Johnston, so that he may find an honourable bread. Farewell, my dear friend. God bless and protect you.

(signed) S. Von Schoultz

To Warren Green, Esq.,
Salina, New York

Note:
Von Schoultz was not buried on Mr. Green's farm, but in St. Mary's Cemetery, Kingston, in a plot owned by the Cicolari family. His grave is immediately behind the vault and is clearly marked.

*Chronicle and Gazette*, Saturday, 8 December 1838

---

## "My Wife!"

*This account from a prisoner of the Rebellion shows that love is stronger than fortifications, even stone ones like Fort Henry.*

At this time a waggon was provided for us, in which we were driven slowly across the Rideau to Fort Henry, followed and accompanied by the Kingston Sheriff, deputy, and jailer, the Niagara deputy and jailer, with a whole division of red coats, carrying arms at present. At the gates of the fort the guard was turned out to receive us, and our entrance was between two platoons of soldiers, which closed after us as if to shut out the hope of ever repassing that barrier. Fort Henry is constructed of good workmanship, on a commanding position, and has an imposing appearance. It is commodiously planned, and has an area of about a half acre, with a large reservoir for water underneath. If well manned, it might hold out against almost any number of assailants ...

We usually had a man stationed at the window about the hour of the customary visits, to report the approach of the officers, when every article of amusement or memento would be put aside; for an order had been issued by the commandant, prohibiting the manufacture of those trifles, fearing they had been, or would be, used as bribes for the sentinel, &c. On the morning of the fourth of November, the man at the window reported the approach of the sheriff, accompanied by two females. My heart fluttered with intense anxiety, while I thrust my face among the dozen the report had brought to the grate, to catch a glimpse of the individuals mentioned, each hoping to discover in them a friend. As soon as I caught a view of the figures, the expression of "my wife!" burst from my lips in deep pathos. In an inordinate tremor of delight, I waited the tardy unlocking of the door, when I found in my embrace the object of all my anxious solicitude but a shadow of mortality. In every lineament of the face were visable traces of care and intense anxiety. Unusual exertion, combined with deep mental distress, had made sad havoc of youth and of health, though the spirit was yet whole and the mind still firm.

The new expression of her affection, despite the dangers of late lake navigation, endeared her more, if possible, to my heart than ever, and I felt, though a prisoner, I would not exchange conditions with the man, though wealthy and free, who had no affection lavished upon him but what his riches purchased. We had but a few minutes for conversation. The sheriff, as soon as he had examined the room, told her to leave, as he must lock the door. However, she stood awhile at the grated window, but not a word must pass without being heard by the guard, or a trifle given without examination. A parcel containing winter clothes, a few pounds of tea, some butter and dried fruit, with a pail of preserves, were cautiously inspected before they could be given up to me. The same conduct was pursued towards Miss Chandler in her communications with her father, in the next ward. Mrs. Wait visited me each morning while I remained, for the sad consolation of fifteen minutes conversation at the window, for subsequent to the first visit, she was debarred entering the door.

Benjamin Wait
*Letters from Van Dieman's Land, Written during Four Years Imprisonment for Political Offences*
Buffalo, 1843

---

## Charles Dickens visits the "bomb-proof fort"

*Charles Dickens visited Kingston for three days in May of 1842, as part of a North American tour. He visited a prisoner of the 1837 Rebellion in Upper Canada, and cast his eyes toward Fort Henry, before travelling on to Montreal by steamboat.*

The time of leaving Toronto for Kingston is noon. By eight o'clock next morning the traveller is at the end of his journey, which is performed by steamboat upon Lake Ontario, calling at Port Hope and Cobourg, the latter a cheerful, thriving little town. Vast quantities of flour form the chief item in the freight of these vessels. We had no fewer than one thousand and eighty barrels on board between Cobourg and Kingston.

The latter place, which is now the seat of government in Canada, is a very poor town, rendered still poorer in the appearance of its market-place by the ravages of a recent fire. Indeed, it may be said of Kingston, that one half of it appears to be burnt down, and the other half not to be built up. The Government House is neither elegant nor commodious, yet it is almost the only house of any importance in the neighbourhood.

There is an admirable jail here, well and wisely governed, and excellently regulated in every respect. The men were employed as shoemakers, ropemakers, Blacksmiths, tailors, carpenters, and stonecutters; and in building a new prison, which was pretty far advanced towards completion. The female prisoners were occupied in needlework. Among them was a beautiful girl of twenty, who had been there nearly three years. She acted as bearer of secret despatches for the self-styled Patriots on Navy Island during the Canadian Insurrection: sometimes dressing as a girl, and carrying them in her stays; sometimes attiring herself as a boy, and secreting them in the lining of her hat. In the latter character she always rode as a boy would, which was nothing to her, for she could govern any horse that any man could ride, and could drive four-in-hand with the best whip in those parts. Setting forth on one of her patriotic missions, she appropriated to herself the first horse she could lay her hands on; and this offence had brought her where I saw her. She had quite a lovely face, though, as the reader may suppose from this sketch of her history, there was a lurking devil in her bright eye, which looked out pretty sharply from between her prison bars.

There is a bomb-proof fort here of great strength, which occupies a bold position, and is capable, doubtless, of doing good service; though the town is much too close upon the frontier to be long held, I should imagine, for its present purpose in troubled times. There is also a small navy-yard, where a couple of Government steamboats were building, and getting on vigorously.

Charles Dickens
*American Notes*
London, 1850

_____

# Martello Tower Disaster

*The Oregon Boundary Dispute of 1846 again raised the spectre of war with the United States. In order to increase Kingston's defences as well as to placate its citizens, six Martello Towers were built in the harbour and at Fort Henry. One evening, a party of workmen returning from the new tower on Cedar Island met with a terrible fate.*

On Saturday evening last a very lamentable accident occurred, by which 17 individuals were hurried into eternity.

A number of workmen employed in the erection of the Martello Tower on Cedar Island, got into a boat, after the termination of their week's labour, for the purpose of crossing to Point Frederick on their return to their homes. We understand the boat was a schooner's jolly-boat, that would have been overloaded with 12 men in her, 23 of these unfortunate individuals, however, crowded into this boat and shoved off. A rather heavy swell was running through the narrow strait they had to cross which on one occasion broke over the boat and wet those on the weather side of it; on the approach of the next wave a number of men suddenly got up for the purpose of avoiding a repetition of their drenching. This movement occasioned an overdue pressure on one side of the overloaded craft, which immediately capsized, bottom up; two of the men saved themselves by swimming, and four others by clinging to the boat until picked up. The remaining 17 were drowned. The following morning all the bodies were recovered, and from the circumstance of some of them being found fast clutched in the hold of others of their fellow sufferers, which even death could not relax, it is conjectured that many, but for this, would have been able to save themselves in a manner similar to that adopted by those who escaped. — Fifteen of those drowned were married men and have left numerous families. It is said that no less than 72 children have by this accident been left destitute.

*Chronicle & Gazette*
Wednesday, 16 September 1846

---

## A Soldier Dies

*The following is a form letter sent from Kingston to the Military Secretary in Montreal. It represents what happened when a British soldier serving in Canada died. It makes provisions for sending the soldier's wife and children to England, and for feeding them until that time.*

Kingston, Canada West
11th October 1861

Sir:
I have the honour to request that the usual rations of provisions may be granted to the Widow and Children (names as per margin) of the Late Private Hugh Donnolly, Royal Canadian Rifles, from the 7th Instant and until an opportunity comes of sending them to England, that being their future place of residence & to which she wishes to be sent as soon as possible.

I have the honour to be
Sir
Your obedient humble servant

F. Walker, Lieutenant Colonel
Commanding, Royal Canadian Rifles

---

## A Plea for Food

*This moving letter was written by an honourable soldier who fell prey to the British soldier's worst enemy — drink. He asks that rations be restored to his family; with his captain vouching for him, it is likely his petition succeeded.*

Patrick Tools to Colonel Bradford, 18 February 1861

Kingston Canada West
18th February 1861

Colonel Bradford

Sir:
I most respectfully take the liberty of soliciting you for your favourable recommendation to the Lieut. General Commanding for the grant of rations to my wife and family. The Privilege of Drawing rations was forfeited by my Rash and unpremeditated misconduct (Desertion caused by a too frequent use of ardent spirits). I respectfully hope and trust Sir that you will be pleased to look over this Criminal act. Having been in possession of two good conduct Badges and wanted only four months to be Entitled to the third — I humbly beg Sir that you would kindly look over any Service Sheets in which you may see that my conduct for 18 1/2 years was that of a good and Deserving Soldier until I fell a victim to Intemperance. But Sir I beg Sincerly to promise that the Remainder of my days in the army Shall Merit for me the name of a Sober well Conducted Soldier — Also Sir I beg to draw your attention to the application which I made to you 18 months past which you kindly told me that as soon as my conduct Deserved the Boon you would recommend one to the consideration of the Lieut. General Commanding for the Restoration of my rations I am happy to State that for the last 16 months I have conducted myself as a well behaved Soldier and for the truth of this Statement Captn. Innes the Captain of my Company has kindly consented to vouch for and to sign his name to this humble application. Again Sir I beg earnestly that you will please to take into consideration the good character of my wife who for the last 14 years has never been brought to the notice of an officer for misconduct and having a Family of 4 Small children to support on my small pay which is not sufficient in conclusion I respectfully and earnstly beg that you will please to Grant this my humble

petition your kind recommendation for the restoration of my rations.

I am Sir your
most obedient Servant
Patrick Toole

---

# Field Exercises and Evolutions of Infantry

*Here is the beginning of the drill manual used by British soldiers in 1867, the time period which the Fort Henry Guard recreates. It emphasises patience, participation, and thoroughness in training recruits.*

## Recruit or Squad Drill

General Principles

I.
1. Instruction of the Recruit.
The instructors to whom this duty is intrusted, must be clear, firm, and concise in their mode of conveying instruction, in order to command attention to their directions. They must allow for the weak capacity of the recruit, and be patient, where endeavour and good-will are apparent, for quickness is the result of practice, and ought not at first to be expected.

2. Recruits must be carried on progressively; they should comprehend one thing before they proceed to another. When first taught their positions, their fingers, elbows, &c., and the rifle, should be properly placed by the instructors; when more advanced, recruits should not be touched, but taught to correct themselves when admonished. They should not be kept too long at any particular part of their exercise. Marching without arms should be intermixed with the rifle instruction.

II.
Duration of Drills, &c.
Short and frequent drills are always to be preferred to long lessons, which exhaust the attention both of the instructor and recruit, and too much pains cannot be taken by those intrusted with the instruction of recruits to move them on progressively from squad to squad according to their merit, so that the quick, intelligent soldier may not be kept back by those of inferior capacity. To arrive at the first squad should be made an object of ambition to the young soldier.

III.
Mutual Instruction.
A system of mutual instruction will be practiced amongst recruits; it gives the young soldier additional interest in his drill, and prepares him for the duties of a non-commissioned officer. Each recruit in succession will occasionally be called out to put his squad through one or two exercises, and encouraged while so doing to correct any error he may observe in the movements of his comrades. If lists of those who show talent for imparting instruction were kept by the captains, and in the orderly room of a regiment, it would be found to create much emulation, and be useful to point out those who were, in this respect, fit for promotion.

---

# Dreams of Desertion

*These stories by a British artilleryman posted to Kingston show desertion attempts could be attended by the supernatural, as well as by farce.*

In the following winter an acquaintance made that night, the senior N.C. Officer of the detachment on Long Island, figured in rather a curious story. When the lake was frozen over desertions to the American side were fairly frequent, and, when these occurred, a signal of two guns for a Royal Artilleryman, and one for other troops, was made from Fort Henry. One of our men, Gunner O'Donoghue, was reported absent and to have started across the ice. There was a good surface, and after mess I started to skate after him, but he had too long a start and it was very dark, so after about an hour's search I gave it up. Those who have skated by night on a big lake are, I imagine, few, and if to the general eeriness of it is added the fact that you are skating after a tolerably strong Irishman who will probably resist being captured as a deserter, it may be realised that, after an hour in which the only sound in the huge expanse of almost total darkness was the swish of my skate blades, my courage began to ooze out of my finger tips, and that it was with a species of shamed relief that I turned and steered straight back for the lights of Fort Henry.

In the early morning the sergeant of the Canadian Rifles, to whom I have already alluded, while out with a search party, found O'Donoghue up to his neck in a pond hole (these are holes in the ice caused by springs in shallow water), and having rescued him with some difficulty, brought him back a prisoner to Fort Henry. The man was tried by court-martial, but while awaiting sentence he escaped from the guard-room, and again received a salute of two guns.

In the evening of the following day I walked into the Canadian Rifle Barracks on my way home from the rink, and saw the sergeant sitting in a sleigh in the courtyard. He saluted and, seeing that he wanted to talk, I went across to him over the snow. "Brought back a prisoner, sergeant? Not O'Donoghue, I hope!" "Well, yes, sir, and if you've a minute to spare, I'd like to tell you about it."

"You will remember," he said, "that last evening the gun went for one of our (Canadian Rifles) men. Well, I took a couple of my men and was out with them for a couple of hours, came back and sent out another patrol in another direction. Then I turned in. Two guns were fired about 1 a.m., and my men came in to report this. Well, sir, I had had a very vivid dream that O'Donoghue had again crossed the lake and had got into the same pond hole. It seemed quite unlikely, of course, but the dream was so strong in me that I sent a couple of men to the place, dressed, and had got about half a mile from our block-house when I met the men coming back with O'Donoghue. They had found him up to his neck and pretty well frozen, and he had got there from another creek, the mouth of which was pretty well a mile away

from the one he came up the first time, but which also led to the same pond hole."

While on the subject of derserters I may mention that the battery we relieved had lost more than a third of their N.C.O.'s and men, desertions being frequent both by boat and over the ice. One of the former excursions had an unexpected end. A bombardier and four men took the officer's four-oar one evening, rowed across the lake, and landed on what they took to be "the other side." They then burned the boat, and cheerily hailed the first civilian they met. "We're deserters from fort 'Enery, we've burnt the officer's boat, and now we want a job in this free country."

"Well," said the man, "I've a friend here, a miller, who wants a few hands; if you come along with me, I daresay he'll take you on." They all strolled down to the block-house, and then the kind civilian, who was the Canadian Rifle N.C.O. of the guard (for obvious reasons these men frequently dressed in plain clothes), made them prisoners, and the next day found them back in Fort 'Enery. We, as a battery, were very proud of ourselves, because during the whole year we were at Kingston we only lost one man, and he bolted the night before we left for Quebec. He was a skillful cabinet-maker and could command large wages in the States; I knew pretty well we should start without him. O'Donoguhue was "dismissed with ignominy from H.M.'s service."

Sir Desmond O'Callaghan, KCVO
*Guns, Gunners, and Others*
London, 1925

———————

## Gunners on the Run

*Desertion was a big problem at Fort Henry, due to the proximity of the American border, as these three successive columns in the local paper make clear.*

Desertion. — On Thursday evening three gunners of the Royal Artillery were missing from Fort Henry at post call. They have not since returned; natural deduction — they have skedaddled. The Government will be relieved of the cost of their transport home, in October next, without doubt.

*Daily British Whig*, May 21, 1870

More Deserters. — The soldiers of the Royal Artillery, at Fort Henry, continue to take out their discharges in a premature and informal manner. Four more deserted on Monday night, and got safely across the river, doubtless, as there are no tidings of their being intercepted. One-fifth of the battery have thus left their posts. The dislike the men entertain towards the expected removal to Bermuda this summer is the incentive to desertion.

*Daily British Whig*, May 26, 1870

Off to Quebec. — Yesterday morning the Battery of Artillery, which has garrisoned Fort Henry for a year or so, left for Quebec in the steamer *Magnet*. It was composed of one officer and (48) men, Dr. Gascoine, Surgeon, accompanying. The small strength of the battery is accounted for in two ways, from the number of recent desertions (about twenty-five), and one officer and 12 men being left behind to take charge of the fort. The orders taking them away were carried out within 24 hours. The battery proceeds to England on Saturday, by the Canadian steamer, and therefore the orders for their transfer to Bermuda have been countermanded. It was this move which the men dreaded, and which led to the desertions. "The girl I left behind me" is disconsolate. Yesterday afternoon at three o'clock the battery of Artillery at Toronto left in the steamer *Spartan*, for Quebec, to embark in the same steamship as the Kingston battery. It passed down early this morning.

*Daily British Whig*, 3 June 1870

---

## End of an Era

*Almost all imperial troops were withdrawn from Canada in the 1870s. This newspaper column notes that 13 men are to be left at Fort Henry.*

The Garrison. — On the 22nd of June Kingston will cease to be a military station, of which it has been the second most important in Canada, if not America, for, we may say, a century. On that day the station must be formally closed, and the garrison will be entrusted to one officer and 12 men, at present quartered in Fort Henry. Mr. West, Barrack Master, is industriously shipping or handing over the stores under his charge, and it is reported that he takes passage for England in the government transport *Crocodile*, on its return. Mr. Rogers, Control officer, remains until October next, in charge of the Military stores at the Dock-yard, and Town Major Mackay is expected to remain until that time also. It is not yet known when the military property will be handed over to the care of the Militia Department here or the Dominion Government.

*Daily British Whig*, 9 June 1870

---

## Bad Treatment Somewhere

*This column, which appeared soon after the Royal Canadian Rifle Regiment was disbanded, evidences what happened to some long serving soldiers who found themselves suddenly thrust out of their life's work with no other prospects.*

On Thursday night an invalided soldier of the R.C. Rifles, very recently discharged, and still wearing the uniform of the corps, applied at the Police Station for protection, being without a lodging for the night, and presumably without means to procure it. He was a fine looking fellow, and was quite sober. His respectable and honest appearance won respect at once, and Serg't Major Robb offered him a night's rest on the bed of one of his own men, instead of in the men's ward, as is customary in regard to night applicants, for which he was grateful. The man is endeavoring to obtain work in the city, and it seems unfeeling that he was not kept on the strength, like very many other soldiers of the corps are, until there was a reasonable prospect of his being able to secure a maintenance. It surely was never intended by the Home Government that a soldier whose peculiar long service almost unfits him for many employments, should be cast adrift objectless and friendless?

*Daily British Whig*, 11 June 1870

## Assasination and Suicide

*In the spring of 1870, a Private took out his grievances against the army in violent manner. Miraculously, his victim survived the attack.*

A frightful occurence took place last evening at the Tete de Pont Barracks. Private Macnamara, of the R. C. Rifles, deliberately shot Colour-Sergeant Thomas Riggs, in his own room, and afterwards placed the revolver to his own head, and fired. Macnamara died in a few minutes. The ball entered under the chin, and passed out through the brain. The murderer met Riggs in a passage, and presented the weapon, and fired. Riggs put up his hand to protect himself, and the ball passed through it, entering his mouth, and passed downwards, and out of the neck. He is in great danger, but it is thought will recover. Medical assistance was at once procured. These are all the particulars which could be obtained in time, owing to the excitement. The assasin and suicide is believed to be insane. Riggs was a very inoffensive man, and no other motive but insanity can be assigned ...

Macnamera was a newly married man, seven and thirty years of age. He volunteered into the corps from the 63rd Regiment, and has seen 16 years service. His wife is at present at Prescott, visiting her parents, and shortly expects to become a mother. Lately the deceased sent her two or three remittances out of his pay, and has corresponded regularly with her during the past week. He was of a morose, dissatisfied nature, and was capable of conceiving intense hatred which he seems to have indulged towards his intended victim deeply. He was seen to dog him in many different places during the day, as if only waiting for a favourable opportunity to carry out the deliberate design expressed in the following letter, which he wrote in the afternoon and left behind in his trunk as an evidence to his true state of mind:

Kingston, Ont., 25 May 1870
I have no wish to say too much on a subject so painful to dwell upon. For the last three years I have not been used as a well-behaved soldier deserved. Both in my daily payment and deposit in the bank, I have been cheated up to my very eyes. I dare not speak about it. In the first place I would not get much satisfaction; in the next, my soldiering would be made miserable. It can be seen that I had enough lately to trouble my mind, without having Sergt. Riggs add more to it. He has confined me for not volunteering. No, not for volunteering, but for spite, or otherwise I would be allowed to judge for myself, as every man in the Regiment was allowed to do. The second time I was confined was a false charge put against me and without hearing what evidence I had to say, punished ... I don't care what people think; I shall if possible, tonight rid the world of the villain, who has caused so much misery to me. All that I am sorry for is that I cannot get one or two others that has always encouraged Serg't Riggs in his villainy in a group; then I would die satisfied. (Signed) Daniel Macnamara

*Daily British Whig*, 26 & 27 May 1870

## A Soldier Honoured

*Despite the hard life and temptations to drink or desert, many soldiers enjoyed long and honourable careers, and some were even recognized formally for it, as this newspaper column makes clear.*

Presentation
The Royal Canadian Rifles paraded at the Tete du Pont Barracks on Friday morning, to witness the presentation of a silver medal with an annuity of £15 a year from the 18th February last to Quarter Master Sergeant Charles Conroy. The regiment having formed square, Adjutant Givens read the order from the Deputy Adjutant General, Montreal, for the presentation to be made in the presence of the regiment, after which Colonel Hibbert complimented Quartermaster Sergeant Conroy on his good luck at the end of his service in having such an honourable distinction bestowed on him, and he knew there was no man in the

regiment more deserving of it. Quartermaster Sergeant Conroy has served nearly 26 years, 21 of which have been as a non-commissioned officer, and he never had a report against him during his whole period of service.

*Daily British Whig*, 31 May 1870

## The Armstrong Gun: the Life of the Party

*When the Northwest Rebellion occurred, Kingston was again swept up in military excitement, most of it more social than martial, as this account relates.*

"... Fort Henry, built in 1832, is still in excellent condition and is the crowning glory of the harbour of Kingston. During the year of the North West Rebellion, the Princess of Wales' Own Rifles, a volunteer regiment of the city, was ordered to garrison Fort Henry for fear of a possible attack from 'American Fenians.' Needless to say, the attack never came, but all during that summer of 1885, old Fort Henry rang with life and merriment. 'The Brave' entertained 'The Fair,' and tennis parties and dances were the order of the day, and deep and earnest was the interest in 'The Armstrong Gun.' To view the 'Armstrong gun' properly it was necessary that the party consist of two — more than two was fatal to the proper appreciation of the beauties of the view from the corner of the ramparts where stood this gun or to the merits of the gun itself ..."

Mary E. Macarow, *Early Days in Kingston, The Cosmos*, October, 1903, Vol. 1, No. 10

## The Poetic Treatment

*Watson Kirkconnel was part of the staff guarding prisoners at Fort Henry during the First World War. He wrote a poem from the perspective of one of the German soldiers kept there; the follow is an excerpt.*

Crumbling Fort Henry, cold and damp,
Became our concentration camp,
Along with several hundred others,

Who hailed us as Germanic brothers.
It was a fortress, old and chill,
Sunk in the summit of a hill
That westward looked on Kingston town
And to the east sloped slowly down
To a deep inlet, bleak and grey,
That bore the name of Dead Man's Bay.
Southward, the broad St. Lawrence reeled;
North, lay the plains of Barriefield.
The fort, I learned, had been erected
A century since, but, long neglected,
Had mouldered with the frost's abuse
Until war claimed its sudden use,
Disturbing in their dank abode,
Spider and beetle, slug and toad.
When Klein and I were landed there,
There'd been scant effort at repair,
For moss was thick upon the roof
And ancient doors were foul with rust
And tottering battlements gave proof
That mortar had dissolved to dust,
While deep along the great dry moat
That hemmed the 'Lower Fort' around
Whole strips of wall had lost a coat
Of ashlars, tumbled on the ground.
But high above, the sentries walked,
Patrolling all the wind-swept hill;
And we, within the ruin, talked,
Or dreamed that we were free men still.

Watson Kirkconnell,
"The Butcher's Tale of the Fort Henry Tunnel," from
*The Flying Bull and Other Tales*, Toronto, 1940

## Kingston Demilitarized

*Fort Henry survives as part of a defence system for Kingston. Not all the parts of this system were so lucky.*

Unfortunately, following the withdrawal of the last Imperial troops in 1870, demolition commenced. In 1875 the inner wall with its guard houses was razed — in fact the stone used in the construction of the house at the entrance to the Royal Military College grounds is part of this inner structure. The space then from the street to the outer wall was converted into what became known as Battery Park, the green grass and sea wall making a fine setting for the City buildings. Here the soldiers paraded on 24th May and Dominion Day, and fire works were set off from the top of the wall, viewed by citizens either ashore or from their row boats and skiffs in the harbour. It also provided a fine place for public receptions, apart from its use as a general recreation place by the youths of the city. Here in 1879, the Marquis of Lorne and Princess Louise were received, when they visited the city to lay the corner stone of the then Arts building of Queen's University. Platforms were erected to seat all the school children, who sang patriotic songs and otherwise took part in the proceedings…

But the hand of the despoiler was to stretch out, grasping this beauty spot in the name of Progress — just as many other historic landmarks have disappeared — those entrusted with the affairs of the people seeing only the immediate advantage, with little thought for the future. With other suitable land going begging, no other site would satisfy, so the remainder of the old Market Battery was destroyed in 1885, and the location given up for railway purposes. The Grand Trunk Railway tracks at that time ran on an embankment situated out in the water, it being possible to enter by openings provided under the tracks and row boats up along the base of the wall … The space between the wall and tracks was filled in with the demolished wall and other debris, only sufficient of the stone being retained to erect the passenger station for the railway — all that remains of a costly and beautiful military work.

E.E. Horsey
"Cataraqui, Fort Frontenac, Kingstown, Kingston"
Kingston, 1937

# Saved from Vandal Hands

*This account from the 1930s shows Fort Henry at its lowest point, just before Ronald Way restored it. It also recounts some popular myths about the fort's orientation and design.*

Henry Hamilton was Lieutenant-Governor, 1782–5; and from Point Henry Fort Henry took its name. A log fort in 1812, a stone one in 1820, preceded the present fort, about which legend has much to tell us; the Duke of Wellington designed the plan, but some clerk sent to Kingston, Jamaica, the plan meant for us and theirs to Kingston, Canada; or it was "built the wrong way round," and that is why a second fort was added, opening out of the first; and so forth. But the Duke's plans were never in the local paper, and experts are less sure than amateurs that the whole thing was a heap of blunders; but here, as elsewhere, the amateurs do most of the talking … The fort dates from 1836, the Martello towers were built ten years later. For forty years now fort and towers have been left to the care of the climate. Perhaps some parts of it were put in order in 1914 when 200 Austrian reservists were interned there. They had tried to travel through southern Ontario on their way from Chicago to New York to sail for Europe, but were invited to leave the train after it had passed under the Detroit river. The wooden roofs of the beautiful Martello towers have rotted or been blown off; frost has done its work on the pointing of the well-built walls; and the Kingston limestone, in spite of local pride, is of poor quality, splitting and cracking in the most lamentable way. At last, and none too soon, the Dominion Government has roused itself to repair the fort, and some day perhaps it will think of the towers. The old block houses are all torn down, the last only a few years ago despite the efforts of General Ross, M.P. for the city, to save it from Vandal hands.

T.R. Glover and D.D. Calvin
*A Corner of Empire*
Cambridge, 1937

# Prime Minister Mackenzie King Opens Fort Henry

*Prime Minister William Lyon Mackenzie King opened the newly restored Fort Henry in August of 1938. The following diary entry shows the strong personal and historical ties he felt to Fort Henry, and how he viewed its importance with regards to the rest of Canada.*

The visit to Fort Henry itself was of exceptional interest. Indeed I shall recall it always as one of the greatest and most significant events of my life. I had, of course, much in mind that father's father had come to Fort Henry in 1836, and confined with the men of the Royal Artillery who came from Aberdeen, the first to be quartered in the Fort when it was sufficiently constructed for purposes of occupation. He lived there a couple of years. It was from there that he went with his battery to the Battle of the Windmill, at Windmill Point, and subsequently went to Fort Wellington at Prescott, where he was working at the time he contracted pneumonia which carried him off later in a hospital at Quebec.

The Fort itself was a great surprise. It has been appropriately called the Western Citadel of Canada, commanding as it does, strategically the entrance to the Great Lakes near the beginning of the St. Lawrence River. Rogers and I were accompanied on our inspection by Brigadier Hertzberg the Officer Commanding the Kingston district, and by Colonel Matthews, head of the R.E.C.

At the Fort, we were met by Mr. Ronald Way, a young man, graduate of Queen's, who has had to do with the work of restoration, an exceptionally able and fine type of man. He took us over a considerable portion of the Fort. We went first through the underground tunnels, along which and from which Montgomery and others who had been taken prisoner with him, at the time of the Rebellion of 1837, made their escape, one of the remarkable incidents of the 1837–38 episode, having prophesied at the time he was sentenced to death, that he would outlive the Judge who pronounced the sentence.

After being shown some of the rooms which have been made into a museum, and now contain different types of arms and equipment used in those days, we were shown some of the quarters in which some of the soldiers were housed. As I stood in one of these rooms, at the far end of the rooms, I witnessed the simplicity of it, the complete absence of anything but the barest necessities of existence, and my thoughts were much of my father's father who at the age of 20, and the years immediately following, no doubt occupied, for some time, possibly the very room which I was being shown. It was interesting to think that I might be walking on the very boards which he, as a young man, had trodden and possibly seeing one of the beds in which he slept, small iron single beds, brought out as part of the ordnance equipment, from the Old World. The front of the stove bore the insignia of George IV reign.

One could not but feel how great an ideal of service men must carry in their breast, who devote their lives to the military career, especially one to be lived in the Spartan simplicity of early colonial days. I much regretted that I had never visited Fort Henry with my father while he was alive ... I felt a great sacredness about everything associated with the Fort, and with the day. It was certainly a part of the Providence of God that I, in the office of Prime Minister, should have been called upon to open this Fort in its restored condition, as a symbol of peace and good-will, after its occupancy, a hundred years ago, by one from whom I am descended, and who was serving the Crown in the stormy period of 1837–1838.

After inspecting part of the Fort, I was taken in the Guard Room, and given the honour of being the first to sign the new guest book which will, from now on, be kept there. It is truly remarkable that it should have fallen to my lot in this year to have opened the Mackenzie home at Queenston, unveiled the Memorial at Niagara, and also, in the same year, to have opened the restored Fort at Kingston, as well as to have participated in the ceremony in commemoration of Von Schultz and his followers at Prescott and to have been given the honour of performing all these ceremonies and to have visited the homes of my ancestors, in Scotland, in the Coronation year, while holding the office of Prime Minister. All this pretty much in the anniversary of the hundred years ...

I was pleased to think while going through the Fort, that the Government of which I am one head, had, as part of the policy which I helped to shape, provided part of the labour and material for the restoration and presortation of this interesting historic national monument. How little could John King, the unknown soldier of 1836, while residing there, have realized that he, through his own strength of character, and what he was imparting of it, was really making all this possible. If parents could only see what their lives can mean to a nation through those who come of their blood, their attitude and outlook towards the affairs of their day would surely be different in may cases, than it is.

There was not time, after we got back to the car, to have more than a bite of lunch; no time to rest. When we reached the Fort for the afternoon ceremonies, at three, we were stopped at the far side of the moat by a question as to who it was that wished to be admitted. The answer given was: The Prime Minister of Canada. The draw-bridge was then lowered, and the doors opened. When we came into the grounds of the Fort, I was received by a guard of honour, first of men drawn up in the uniform of the early days; subsequently, another guard of honour, war veterans, both of which guards were inspected. There was an enormous crowd in the arena, in the galleries, and on the walls. The high wind and threatening storm made it a difficult day for speaking. On the platform were: Colonel Mills, the Chairman; Rogers, the Federal Minister of Labour; Colin Campbell, Provincial Minister of Public Works; General Hertzberg, and myself ...

After the morning ceremony, I had a few words with Mrs. Henderson; also with an old lady who had been born in the Fort 90 years ago. Before the completion of the ceremony, Rogers, Smith, and myself were each presented with a small cannon as souvenirs of the occasion. They were reproductions of those used in the early days, and the wood was from one of the original mountings. I should not be surprised if it may have been from one of the cannons with which my father's father had to do either in training at the Fort, or on service during the Rebellion period. The numbers being as few as they were, the probabilities are very great that such was the case.

When the ceremonies were over, there was only time for a change of dress, and a minute or two's rest before returning to the LaSalle Hotel where a dinner in my honour was given by those who had to do with the centennial celebrations, particularly the proceedings at the Fort.

The dinner was presided over by Mr. Nickle, a brother of the Honourable Mr. Nickle, ex-M.P., who, as a member of the City Council, acted in the absence of the Mayor who had been called to Toronto through a death in his family. It was a fine gathering representative of citizens of Kingston, many ex-Mayors being present and leading civic officials. Nickle made an exceedingly good speech referring in exceptionally generous terms to Rogers and to the Government. While very tired, I felt much more at ease at the dinner than I had felt at the afternoon gathering, and was able to say a few things which helped to compensate for what had been omitted in the afternoon speech. However, the place for them would have been at the Fort and at the time of the broadcast, particularly references to Mr. Way and Mr. McQuesten ...

After the dinner, we attended a pageant, reviewing historical events connected with Kingston. I shall never forget the sight of the Fort that night. In its way, it was as wonderful as the sight of Riverdale Park on the previous afternoon. Rogers spoke of the resemblance to the Coliseum in the days of ancient Rome. It seemed to combine the best that Rome and Greece had ever exhibited in their day. The outline of the figures of people on the walls as the lights were thrown upon them, with the dark sky beyond, was as beautiful as anything I have ever seen in my life. The first part of the pageant was very good; the latter part, poor, and dragged considerably. There were historical inaccuracies as, for example, mention of Mackenzie as being responsible for Von Schultz' execution, something he never had anything to do with. There continued to be glorification of Tory loyalty to the Crown at the expense of the Liberal loyalty to principle of true democracy and liberty.

The moon shone brightly in the sky during part of the evening performance, and when all was over, the heavens were lit up with the beauty of Northern lights. I was escorted from the Fort by the Fort Henry guards, a body of young men in sweater uniform. The drive from the Fort to the City was something never to be forgotten. Looking back to the line of motor cars coming down the hill side was as though the whole place had been especially lighted for the occasion. When I got back to my car, I felt the night had closed in on the day in my life, in some way, more filled with memories of historic interest and family association than any other, excepting the day at Niagara. I was very sad at heart that I should have failed to have been equal to its opportunities, but grateful to God that I had been spared to immediate to those to whose character I owe all that in me is of any worth to my country. Colonel Hills, Major Nickle, Mr. and Mrs. Rogers, Colonel Scott joined Handy and myself in a little late supper after returning to the car.

It was about one when we turned in.

National Archives of Canada, William Lyon Mackenzie King Papers, MG 26 J13, Diaries Series, 1 August 1938, microfiche T-124 (transcript series), p. 584-590 (typewritten p. 760-766).

------

# Ronald Lawrence Way: the Father of Historic Restoration in Canada

*The following text is excerpted from a previously unpublished essay by Stephen Mecredy on Ronald Way.*

During a speech to the Annual Meeting of the Canadian Historical Association in June 1960, Ronald Way stated:

> *If I have a personal mission it is been to sell Canada to Canadians. It is our history, only, which makes Canadians different from the Americans who share the environment of this continent …The justification of our living museums of history, whether military or social, lies in their interpretation of Canadian history to the average person.*

Ronald Way could be called the father of historic restoration in Canada. Although there were some minor attempts in the field of preservation before the restoration of Fort Henry (1936–38), the fort marked the beginning of a significant movement to protect Canada's heritage. This can be seen in the restoration of Fort York in Toronto and the Halifax Citadel in Nova Scotia during the same time period …

Ronald Way was born January 2, 1908, in Kingston, the son of a Queen's graduate (M.Sc.). The family moved to Ottawa when he was a child but returned to Kingston in the 1920s following the early death of his father, who was an engineer. Following his father's wishes, he enrolled in Applied Science (Engineering) at Queen's, but switched to Arts in his second year because of his love for the study of history. His aptitude for engineering, however, was to stand him in good stead in later years when so much of his work involved building techniques and reconstruction.

At Queen's he continued in history, graduating in 1936 with an Honours M.A. in History and English. He won several scholarships including the Western Ontario Graduate Fellowship. His Master's thesis was on the fortifications in the Niagara Peninsula during the War of 1812. Soon after the completion of his studies, this knowledge of fortifications lead him to work in the area of historic restoration with dramatic results …

Ronald Way fell naturally into the job of Director of Restoration as he was working on his Master's in history at Queen's University. For two years he ate, slept and dreamt Fort Henry, even living there for some time. The job was immense and involved tearing down decayed limestone walls, restoring what was behind them and rebuilding the walls with the original stone or fresh cut stone when the original was too badly damaged. Fort Henry was the first large scale restoration in Canada. At one time, over 300 men were employed and the time limit placed on the work of having to open August 1, 1938, put a terrific strain on Way.

It is remarkable that during the hectic period of restoration he should find the time to create another first in museum interpretation — living history in the form of the Fort Henry Guard. It was originally just an historian's dream — to bring back the soldiers who once garrisoned the fort to breathe life into the inanimate fortress. Ronald Way made his dream a reality by hiring, clothing and drilling a small group of university and high school students in 1938. Way managed to convince the Department of National Defence to "lend" him a large number of obsolete weapons and uniforms from the 1885 period which he used to clothe the first Fort Henry Guard. This tiny band of twenty-three "interpreters" in a motley collection of original uniforms and equipment, formed a Guard of Honour for Prime Minister William Lyon Mackenzie King. He opened the fort to the public "…in the name of those unknown British soldiers who laid the foundation of this land" on August 1, 1938. Way's was a work of genius in the creation of what is now called "living history" …

Almost immediately following the restoration of Fort Henry, Ronald Way was called upon to supervise the restoration of Fort George in Niagara-on-the-Lake, Fort Erie in Fort Erie, William Lyon Mackenzie House in Queenston and Joseph Brant House in Burlington. All through this time Way continued as Director of Fort Henry which was open in the summer of 1939 and part of 1940.

When World War II closed Fort Henry, Ronald Way tried to enlist in the Army; he was rejected on medical grounds. Sent to the Niagara Parks Commission by the Ontario government, he worked on historic projects in the area and wrote the definitive history of the Commission's first fifty years. This period in his life was very important because while he was in Niagara he met and married Beryl (Taffy) Way. She became his executive assistant, constant companion and confidant, and also acted as his associate in his work from that point on.

After the war, Way was forced to restore Fort Henry once again after the military vacated the premises for the fort had been used as an internment camp during the war for German merchant seamen as well as soldiers and airmen. The Department of National Defence and the Ontario government could not agree who was to pay for the refurbishing of the fort, consequently it was 1948 before Fort Henry was once again reopened as a museum and historic site. Way often commented that it cost more to restore Fort Henry after World War II than it did in 1938! He was right, since it cost close to one million dollars to complete the project a second time.

After the fort was opened as a museum for the second time [in 1948], Way turned his energies to perfecting the living history aspect of the site — the Fort Henry Guard. Over the next half dozen years, great efforts were made to make the Guard as authentic as possible to the year 1867 in its dress and drill. The Guard's uniform and equipment were researched and prototypes made so suppliers could make accurate reproductions. The culmination of this work was the visit of the Guard to Marine Barracks, Washington D.C. in the summer of 1955 and the Guard's participation in the 1956 Royal Tournament in London, England. The Fort Henry Guard has celebrated July 1, Dominion Day, annually since 1939 and is uniformed, equipped and performs the drill for the year 1867, Canada's Confederation year.

In 1958 Way began his second great project. He was appointed Director of Historic Sites for the St. Lawrence Parks Commission and in addition to directing Fort Henry, he was in charge of the restoration of Upper Canada Village. For the next three years he travelled constantly between Morrisburg and Kingston. His experience in restoration and interpretation were invaluable to the project and Upper Canada Village was heralded as the finest outdoor history museum in North America soon after it opened.

By now his reputation was such that in 1961 the Federal Government asked for a "loan" of his services (and those of Mrs. Way) to get the Fortress of Louisbourg project off the ground. From 1962 to 1967 Way held the post of General Consultant and Chief of Research at Louisbourg while at the same time continuing as Director of Historic Sites for the Parks Commission. He made nearly 100 trips to the Maritimes, (practically twice a month) which severely affected his health.

He retired from the Ontario Civil Service in 1965 continued to act as a consultant for some years after that. In 1973 Way was awarded the Order of Canada for his outstanding contribution to Canadian historic restoration and in 1974, his alma mater, Queen's University at Kingston, awarded him an honourary doctorate of laws degree. It says much for the man that he was seriously contemplating beginning work on a Ph.D. in history at that time. Ronald L. Way died in November 1978, aged seventy …

Ronald Lawrence Way, in his own words, made Canadians take "a sugar coated pill of history" each time they visited Fort Henry, Upper Canada Village, Louisbourg and any of the other restorations he worked on. We all have been better Canadians because of him.

# RECOMMENDED READING

Chartrand, René. *Canadian Military Heritage*. V. II. Montreal: Art Global, 1993.

Farwell, Byron. *Mr. Kipling's Army*. London: W.W. Norton and Company, 1981.

Featherstone, Donald. *Weapons and Equipment of the Victorian Soldier*. Dorset: Blandford Press, 1978.

Luciuk, Luboymer, *A Time for Atonement*. Kingston: The Limestone Press, 1988.

Osborne, Brian S. and Swainson, Donald. *Kingston: Building on the Past*. Westport: Butternut Press, 1988.

Smith, A. Britton, ed. *Kingston, Oh Kingston!* Kingston: Brown & Martin, 1987

Trustram, Myna. *Women of the Regiment: Marriage and the Victorian Army*. Cambridge: Cambridge University Press, 1984.

Walter, John. ed. *Arms and Equipment of the British Army, 1866*. London: Greenhill Books, 1986.

Whitfield, Carol. *Tommy Atkins: The British Soldier in Canada, 1759 to 1870*. Ottawa: Ministry of the Environment, 1981.

Wolseley, Colonel G.J. *The Soldier's Pocket-Book for Field Service*. London: Macmillan and Co., 1869.

**Articles:**

Lee, David. "The Battle of the Windmill" in *History and Archaeology*. No. 8. Ottawa: Ministry of Supply and Services, 1976.

Patterson, William J. "Fort Henry: Military Mistake or Defiant Deterrent" in *Historic Kingston*, 1983.

# INDEX